Anonymous

Narrative of Privations and Sufferings of United States Officers and Soldiers

while prisoners of war. Being the report of a commission of inquiry, appointed by the United States sanitary commission. Vol. 1

Anonymous

Narrative of Privations and Sufferings of United States Officers and Soldiers
while prisoners of war. Being the report of a commission of inquiry, appointed by the United States sanitary commission. Vol. 1

ISBN/EAN: 9783337308001

Printed in Europe, USA, Canada, Australia, Japan

Cover: Foto ©ninafisch / pixelio.de

More available books at **www.hansebooks.com**

NARRATIVE

OF

PRIVATIONS AND SUFFERINGS

OF

UNITED STATES OFFICERS & SOLDIERS

WHILE

PRISONERS OF WAR

IN THE HANDS OF

THE REBEL AUTHORITIES.

BEING

THE REPORT OF A COMMISSION OF INQUIRY, APPOINTED BY THE UNITED STATES SANITARY COMMISSION.

WITH AN APPENDIX,
CONTAINING THE TESTIMONY.

"*For I was an hungred, and ye gave Me no meat; I was thirsty, and ye gave Me no drink; I was a stranger, and ye took Me not in; naked, and ye clothed Me not; sick, and in prison, and ye visited Me not.*"

"*Lord, when saw we Thee an hungred, or athirst, or a stranger, or naked, or sick, or in prison, and did not minister unto Thee?*"

"*Verily I say unto you, inasmuch as ye did it not to one of the least of these, ye did it not to Me.*"

MEMBERS OF THE COMMISSION.

VALENTINE MOTT, M.D., LL.D.,
Ex-President of the Medical Department of the University of New York, and Emeritus Professor of Surgery; Fellow of King and Queen's College of Physicians of Ireland; Honorary Fellow of the Royal Medical and Chirurgical Society of London, etc., etc. *Chairman of the Commission.*

EDWARD DELAFIELD, M.D.,
President of the College of Physicians and Surgeons of New York, and Emeritus Professor of Obstetrics and the Diseases of Women and Children; President of the National Ophthalmological Society, etc., etc.

GOUVERNEUR MORRIS WILKINS, Esq.

ELLERSLIE WALLACE, M.D.,
Professor of Obstetrics and the Diseases of Women and Children, Jefferson Medical College, Philadelphia, etc.

HON. J. I. CLARK HARE,
Judge of the District Court of the City and County of Philadelphia.

REV. TREADWELL WALDEN,
Rector of St. Clement's Church, Philadelphia.

PUBLISHED AT THE OFFICE OF "LITTELL'S LIVING AGE," BOSTON.

PRICE TWENTY CENTS.

EXTRACTS

FROM THE

MINUTES OF PROCEEDINGS OF THE STANDING COMMITTEE OF THE UNITED STATES SANITARY COMMISSION.

823 BROADWAY, NEW YORK, May 19, 1864.

Resolved, That Dr. ELLERSLIE WALLACE, Hon. J. I. CLARK HARE, and the Rev. TREADWELL WALDEN, of Philadelphia, and Dr. VALENTINE MOTT, Dr. EDWARD DELAFIELD, and GOUVERNEUR M. WILKINS, Esq., of New York, be respectfully requested to act as a Commission for ascertaining, by inquiry and investigation, the true physical condition of prisoners, recently discharged by exchange, from confinement at Richmond and elsewhere, within the rebel lines; whether they did, in fact, during such confinement, suffer materially for want of food, or from its defective quality, or from other privations or sources of disease; and whether their privations and sufferings were designedly inflicted on them by military or other authority of the Rebel Government, or were due to causes which such authorities could not control. And that the gentlemen above named be requested to visit such camps of paroled or discharged prisoners as may be accessible to them, and to take, in writing, the depositions of so many of such prisoners as may enable them to arrive at accurate results; and to adopt such other means of investigation as they may think proper.

823 BROADWAY, NEW YORK, May 31, 1864.

Voted, to request of the Committee of Investigation on the condition of exchanged Union prisoners, the examination not only of Union prisoners, but also of some of the Rebel prisoners recently captured, with reference to the question whether they have, while in the Confederate service, suffered like privations to those experienced by the Federal captives.

The above is a correct copy from the Minutes.

J. FOSTER JENKINS,
General Secretary of the United States Sanitary Commission.

September, 1864.

The Commissioners appointed in the foregoing resolution, by the Standing Committee of the United States Sanitary Commission, respectfully submit the following Narrative and Report—drawn from the mass of evidence collected by them, and printed in the Appendix—as the result of their inquiry and investigation.

V. MOTT,
EDWD. DELAFIELD,
GOUV. MOR. WILKINS,
ELLERSLIE WALLACE,
J. I. CLARK HARE,
TREADWELL WALDEN.

COPIES

OF

PHOTOGRAPHS OF UNION SOLDIERS

AFTER THEIR RETURN FROM

IMPRISONMENT AT BELLE ISLE.

Accurately copied from the Original Photographs taken at United States General Hospital, Division No. 1, Annapolis, Maryland, and now in the possession of the United States Sanitary Commission.

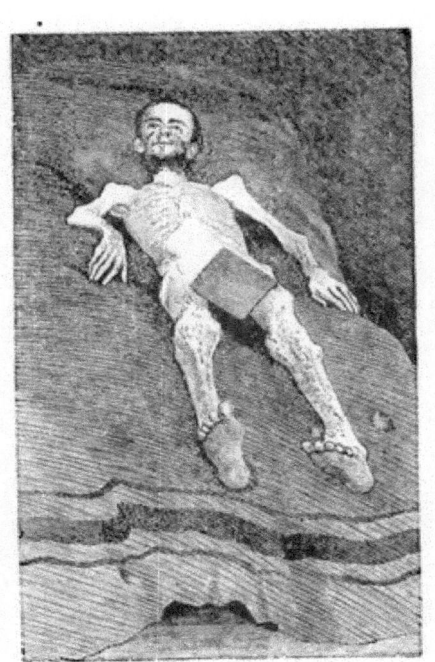

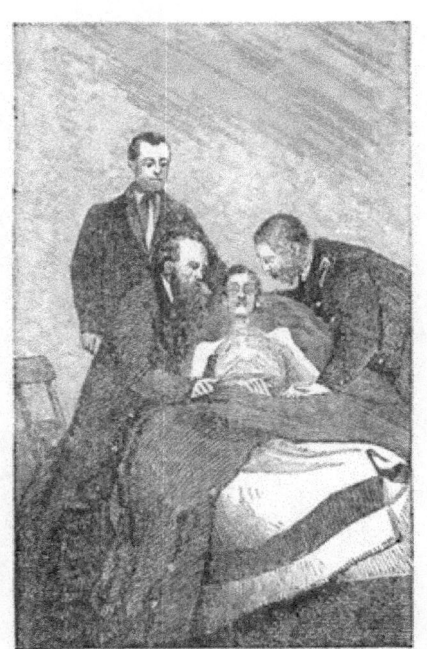

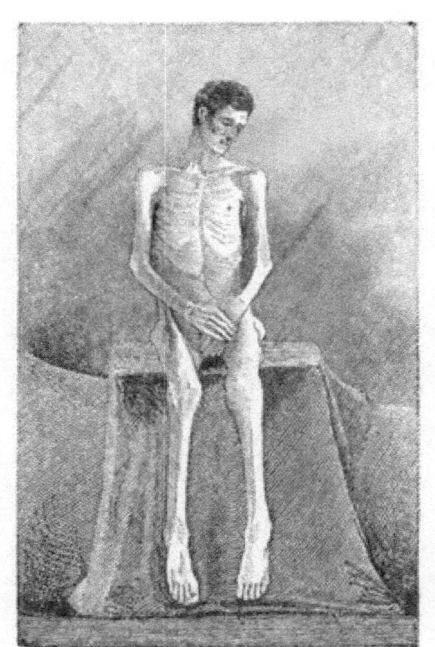

THE NARRATIVE AND REPORT OF THE COMMISSION.

I.

Reports of Cruelties in the Beginning of the War — Mutual Recrimination of North and South — Later and more Authentic Reports — Heart-rending Condition of Returned Prisoners — The Congressional Inquiry — The Sanitary Commission Appoints a Commission of Inquiry — Range of the Investigation — Visit of the Commissioners to Annapolis and Baltimore — Appearance of the Returned Prisoners — Living Skeletons — Testimony Taken — The Claim of the Rebel Government and People — The Humane Principles of Modern Warfare.

EVER since the outbreak of the war, the country has been full of painful rumors concerning the treatment of prisoners of war by the rebel authorities. Every returned prisoner has brought his tale of suffering, astonishing his neighborhood with an account of cruelty and barbarity on the part of the enemy. Innumerable narratives have also been published and widely circulated.

The public have been made very uneasy by these reports. One class have accepted them as true; another have felt them to be exaggerated; still another have pronounced them wholly false,—fictions purposely made and scattered abroad to inflame the people against their enemies, and doing great injustice to the South.

On the other hand, rumors have crossed the border, of an outraged public sentiment in the South, precisely on the same account: reports abounding there of cruelty and barbarity to the rebel soldiers in our hands. It has been repeatedly announced that whatever restrictions or privations have been suffered by Northern men in Southern prisons, were in retaliation for these.

In the beginning of such a prodigious contest, as this has proved to be, breaking out in the midst of a people unaccustomed to war, and quite removed from extensive military traditions and examples, it was natural that many irregularities should have occurred, and many usages of warfare been disregarded on both sides; and that in the matter of prisoners especially, where either region was suddenly inundated by many thousands, great abuses should have taken place, until accommodations could be provided, and arrangements perfected.

But these early days of ill-preparation have long passed away. The war has lasted more than three years. Both sections have become accustomed to it, and are familiarized with the ideas, habits, and laws of military life. The passionate fury of one side and the patriotic indignation of the other, have had time to settle down, at least so far as to accept this condition, and make every civilized provision known in modern warfare, for the mitigation of its horrors and inhumanity.

And yet the painful rumors, so rife at the outbreak of the war, instead of subsiding with its early tumult, have lately increased to an extent which has seriously alarmed and aroused the public. The tales of cruelty and suffering have become even more heart-rending. Months ago we heard reports that our men were starving and freezing in the Southern prisons. In the late temporary resumption of the cartel, boat-loads of half-naked living skeletons, foul with filth, and covered with vermin, were said to have been landed at Annapolis and Baltimore. Men, diseased and dying, or physically ruined for life, unfit for further military service, had been received in the stead of soldiers of the enemy returned in good condition, and who had been well fed, well clothed, and well sheltered by our Government during their captivity.

But many reasons were circulated to account for such a difference. It was alleged that these emaciated men were the victims of camp dysentery, or similar distempers, and of food, which, however good in quality, and sufficient in quantity, was averse to the Northern constitution. Again it was alleged that the rebel army was, itself, suffering for want of food and clothing, and that the very guards to these prisoners had fared no better.

There were many among us who were willing to credit any statement which would mitigate or excuse the infamy of permitting such a condition of things. For the sake of humanity and the American name, they hoped that the worst could not be proved.

But there were others to whom the proof was sufficient, and who were convinced that the whole was a horrible and pre-determined scheme, contrived for the purpose of depleting our armies, and discouraging our soldiers.

The attention of Congress was roused, and a committee was appointed to investigate this and other alleged barbarities. Their report has just been published.

Before, however, the result of their inquiries was known, the United States Sanitary Commission, as the organ of popular humanity and philanthropy, determined to make an independent investigation; and such a one as would, if possible, put the question at rest on all points upon which the public mind was divided or unsettled; and furnish information so full, and so direct from original sources, that every one could arrive at a just conclusion.

They accordingly appointed the undersigned as a Commission of Inquiry, partly because they were known to be removed from any political affiliations and prejudices, and partly because three of their number were supposed to be professionally competent to read the unerring testimony of nature in the physical condition of the men.

Two distinct departments of evidence were thus opened.

In entering upon their duties the Commissioners had no other wish than to ascertain the truth, and to report the facts as they were. For this they endeavored to collect all the evidence within their reach, and to hear and record all that could be said on every side of the subject. They were accompanied by a United States Commissioner, and in every case the testimony was taken on oath or affirmation before him, or in his absence, before other officers equally empowered.

The mass of evidence, printed as an Appendix, was collected during a period of several months, and is now arranged and classified to facilitate the reader's reference. If it had been printed in the order in which it was taken, it would have been too irregular and apparently heterogeneous to have exhibited the total result of the investigation. But, as it now stands, it will be found united and homogeneous enough in the tragical story which it tells, without variation or self-contradiction, to the country and to the world.

Much of the evidence, however, is made up of bare abstracts of the free and full conversations that were held with persons examined, and although all the essential facts are preserved, yet many graphic and pathetic minor details are omitted which escaped, or could not enter, the formal record, but sometimes were noted down by those who were present. Besides this, the Commissioners were witnesses themselves, and saw and heard enough to overwhelm them with astonishment, and remove the last doubt from their minds.

For this reason, and that the reader may share with them, so far as can be, the almost dramatic development of the inquiry, they send out these pages, not in the form of a brief documentary report, simply referring to the testimony, but as a descriptive narrative, in which all the salient points of the evidence, and the results of their own observation, are incorporated together. Such a narrative need be only an intelligible grouping of material—its facts will speak best for themselves.

The Commissioners, at the very outset, were brought face to face with the returned captives.

They first visited the two extensive hospitals in Annapolis, occupying the spacious buildings and grounds of the Naval Academy and St. John's College, where over three thousand of them had been brought in every conceivable form of suffering, direct from the Libby Prison, Belle Isle, and two or three other Southern military stations.[*]

They also visited the West's Buildings Hospital and the Jarvis General Hospital in Baltimore, where several hundreds had been brought, in an equally dreadful condition.

The photographs of these diseased and emaciated men, since so widely circulated, painful as they are, do not, in many respects, adequately represent the sufferers as they then appeared.

The best picture cannot convey the reality, nor create that startling and sickening sensation which is felt at the sight of a human skeleton, with the skin drawn tightly over its skull, and ribs, and limbs, weakly turning and moving itself, as if still a living man!

And this was the reality.

The same spectacle was often repeated as the visitors went from bed to bed, from ward to ward, and from tent to tent. The bony faces stared out above the counterpanes, watching the passer-by dreamily and indifferently. Here and there lay one, half over upon his face, with his bed clothing only partially dragged over him, deep in sleep or stupor. It was strange to find a Hercules in bones; to see the immense hands and feet of a young giant pendent from limbs thinner than a child's, and that could be spanned with the thumb and finger! Equally strange and horrible was it to come upon a man, in one part shrivelled to nothing but skin and bone, and in another swollen and misshapen with dropsy or scurvy; or further on, when the

[*] The Commissioners would acknowledge the courtesy and hospitality of the accomplished and efficient Surgeon in charge of the Hospital at the Naval Academy, Dr. VanderKieft, by whom every facility for conducting the inquiry was heartily given.

surgeon lifted the covering from a poor half-unconscious creature, to see the stomach fallen in, deep as a basin, and the bone protruding through a blood-red hole on the hip.

Of course these were the worst cases among those that still survived. Hundreds like them, and worse even than they, had been already laid in their graves.

The remainder were in every gradation of physical condition. Some were able to sit up, and to move feebly around their bed; others were well enough to be out of doors; many were met walking about the beautiful grounds of the Naval Academy—by a curious and probably accidental compensation, on the part of the Government, swung to this Paradise on the Severn from the sandy little island in James river and its bleak and bitter winds.

But however unlike and various the cases were, there was one singular element shared by all, and which seemed to refer them to one thing as the common cause and origin of their suffering. It was the peculiar look in every face. The man in Baltimore looked like the man just left in Annapolis. Perhaps it was partly the shaven head, the sunken eyes, the drawn mouth, the pinched and pallid features—partly, doubtless, the grayish, blighted skin, rough to the touch as the skin of a shark. But there was something else: an expression in the eyes and countenance of desolateness, a look of settled melancholy, as if they had passed through a period of physical and mental agony which had driven the smile from their faces forever. All had it: the man that was met on the grounds, and the man that could not yet raise his head from the pillow.

It was this which arrested the attention of some of the party quite as much as the remarkable phenomenon of so many emaciated and singularly diseased men being gathered together, all, with few exceptions, having been brought from the same prisons in the South.

Every one who was questioned contributed his part to swell the following account of privation, exposure and suffering.

The veil is now to be lifted from two of the nearest and most noted Southern stations for prisoners. There appear, indeed, occasional glimpses of places of captivity in Danville, Virginia, and Andersonville, Georgia, but the chief interest centres upon Libby Prison and Belle Isle, at Richmond.

Before, however, the narrative proceeds, two things must be borne in mind:

First, that we are now penetrating into the arrangements of a people who claim, and have so far maintained, their entire independence of the United States Government; who have organized a government of their own; who have also organized immense and powerful armies; who had, in the beginning, so far prepared themselves, and, during the last three years, have so far completed their preparations, as to be able to match, and all but overpower one of the strongest military establishments ever known.

Let them, for the moment, be taken for what they claim to be: "The Confederate States of America," a mighty government, and a "superior race," first in civilization, in culture, and in courage, distinguished for all that is magnanimous, chivalric, humane, hospitable, and noble, for all the graces and refinements, and highest developments of individual and social life.

Furthermore, another thing must be borne in mind: that, in these days of civilized warfare, the cowardly and barbarous usage no longer prevails of maltreating prisoners of war, but the moment a conflict is over, every sentiment of Christianity and humanity rises to mitigate the bloody horrors of the field. The distinction of friend and enemy is no longer known.

The surgeon, with the high sense of professional duty in which he has been educated, goes equally to all. The prisoners taken are not thrown into dungeons, nor shut up in jails, but put into barracks. They are made as comfortable as the arrangements necessary for their safe keeping will permit. They are sheltered, warmed, fed and clothed, in all necessary respects as well as the soldiers that vanquished and captured them. They become, for the time being, part of the military family of their enemy, and are made subject to the same sanitary and other regulations.

Their barracks are never overcrowded; sufficient area is allowed for exercise and fresh air; so much bathing is permitted, and even insisted upon, for the sake of cleanliness; their food is in every respect the same as that consumed by the army within whose lines they are; their clothing is all that they need. Such a thing as robbery of their private property is unknown, or never tolerated if known.

When sickness overtakes the prisoner he is removed to the hospital: taken from his bunk and placed upon a bed, and then, whatever distinction existed before vanishes entirely: every kindness and attention, every remedy and delicacy that a sufferer needs, is freely and generously given.

Such is the high principle, and noble usage, which prevails in modern warfare. The perfection of its arrangements is a matter of pride and honor among soldiers, and the proper boast of every Christian government.

We now turn to the people and government at present waging war with our Government, and who, through a dead-lock in the cartel, hold tens of thousands of United States soldiers as prisoners of war.

II.

Almost invariable Robbery of Prisoners—Description of Libby Prison—Overcrowded Rooms—Barely room to lie down—Ragged and verminous Blankets—Shooting at prisoners without warning—Instances of Shooting in Libby—Same in Danville and Atlanta—Insufficient and disgusting Rations—Slow Starvation—Withholding and thieving of Boxes sent from the North—Sufferings of the Officers—The Cells—Inhumanity to the Dead—The Mining of Libby.

THE first fact developed by the testimony of both officers and privates, is that prisoners were almost invariably robbed of everything valuable in their possession, sometimes on the field, at the instant of capture, sometimes by the prison authorities in a "quasi official way," with the promise of return when exchanged or paroled; but which promise was never fulfilled.* This robbery amounted often to a stripping of the person of even necessary clothing. Blankets and overcoats were almost always taken, and sometimes other articles; in which case damaged or ragged ones were returned in their stead.

This preliminary over, the captives were taken to prison.

The Libby, which is best known, though also used as a place of confinement for private soldiers, is generally understood to be the officers' prison.

It is a row of brick buildings, three stories high, situated on the canal, and overlooking the James river, and was formerly a tobacco warehouse. The partitions between the buildings have been pierced with doorways on each story.

The rooms are one hundred feet long by forty feet broad. In six of these rooms, twelve hundred United States officers, of all grades, from the Brigadier-General to the Second-Lieutenant, were confined for many months; and this was all the space that was allowed them in which to cook, eat, wash, sleep, and take exercise! It seems incredible. Ten feet by two were all that could be claimed by each man—hardly enough to measure his length upon; and even this was further abridged by the room necessarily taken for cooking, washing and clothes-drying.

* No instance of the promise being kept appears in the evidence, but there have been occasions reported, though very rare, where money was returned, but even then in depreciated Confederate currency.

At one time they were not allowed the use of benches, chairs or stools, nor even to fold their blanket and sit upon them, but those who would rest were obliged to huddle on their haunches, as one of them expresses it, "like so many slaves on the middle passage." After awhile this severe restriction was removed, and they were allowed to make chairs and stools for themselves, out of the barrels and boxes which they had received from the North.

They were overrun with vermin in spite of every precaution and constant ablutions. Their blankets, which averaged one to a man, and sometimes less, had not been issued by the rebels, but had been procured in different ways; sometimes by purchase, sometimes through the Sanitary Commission. The prisoners had to help themselves from the refuse accumulation of these articles, which, having seen similar service before, were often ragged and full of vermin.

In these they wrapped themselves at night, and lay down on the hard plank floor in close and stifling contact, "wormed and dovetailed together," as one of them testifies, "like fish in a basket." The floors were recklessly washed late in the afternoon, and were therefore damp and dangerous to sleep upon. Almost every one had a cough in consequence.

There were seventy-five windows in these rooms, all more or less broken, and in winter the cold was intense. Two stoves in a room, with two or three armfuls of wood to each, did not prove sufficient, under this exposure, to keep them warm.

The regulations varied at different periods in stringency and severity, and it is difficult to describe the precise condition of things at any one time, but the above comes from two officers, Lieutenant-Colonel Farnsworth and Captain Calhoun. As it happens, they are representatives of the two opposite classes of officers confined in the Libby. The former coming from Connecticut, and influentially connected at the North, was one of a mess to which a great profusion of supplies, and even luxuries, were sent. The latter coming from Kentucky, and being differently situated, was entirely dependent upon the prison fare.

These officers were there during the same season, but never became acquainted. The accounts of each, which will be found in the evidence side by side, are here combined and run together.

From their statements it appears that the hideous discomfort was never lessened by any variation in the rules, but often increased. The prison did not seem to be under any general and uniform army regulations, but the captives were subject to the caprices of

Major Turner, the officer in charge, and Richard Turner, inspector of the prison.

It was among the rules that no one should go within three feet of the windows, a rule which seems to be general in all Southern prisons of this character and which their frequently crowded state rendered peculiarly severe and difficult to observe. The manner in which the regulation was enforced was unjustifiably and wantonly cruel. Often by accident, or unconsciously, an officer would go near a window, and be instantly shot at without warning. The reports of the sentry's musket were heard almost every day, and frequently a prisoner fell either killed or wounded.

It was even worse with a large prison near by, called the Pemberton Buildings, which was crowded with enlisted men. The firing into its windows was a still more common occurrence. The officers had heard as many as fourteen shots fired on a single day. They could see the guards watching for an opportunity to fire, and often, after one of them had discharged his musket, the sergeant of the guard would appear at the door, bringing out a dead or wounded soldier.

So careless as this were the authorities as to the effect of placing their prisoners in the power of the rude and brutal soldiery on guard. It became a matter of sport among the latter "to shoot a Yankee." They were seen in attitudes of expectation, with guns cocked, watching the windows for a shot. But sometimes they did not even wait for an infraction of the rule. Lieutenant Hammond was shot at while in a small boarded enclosure, where there was no window, only an aperture between the boards. The guard caught sight of his hat through this opening, and aiming lower, so as to reach his heart, fired. A nail turned the bullet upward, and it passed through his ear and hat-brim. The officers reported the outrage to Major Turner, who merely replied, "The boys are in want of practice." The sentry said, "He had made a bet that he would kill a damned Yankee before he came off guard." No notice was taken of the occurrence by the authorities.

The brutal fellow, encouraged by this impunity, tried to murder another officer in the same way. Lieutenant Huggins was standing eight feet from the window, in the second story. The top of his hat was visible to the guard, who left his beat, went out into the street, took deliberate aim, and fired. Providentially he was seen, a warning cry was uttered. Huggins stooped, and the bullet buried itself in the beams above.

Very much the same thing is mentioned as happening in the prison buildings at Danville. A man was standing by the window conversing with private Wilcox. At his feet was the place where he slept at night, close under the window, and where his blanket lay rolled up. He had his hand on the casement. The guard must have seen his shadow, for he was invisible from the regular beat, and went out twenty feet to get a shot at him. Before the poor fellow could be warned, the bullet entered his forehead, and he fell dead at the feet of his companion.

Almost every prisoner had such an incident to tell. Some had been shot at themselves a number of times, and had seen others repeatedly fired upon. One testifies that he had seen five hundred men shot at.

The same brutal style of "sporting" while on guard, seems to have prevailed wherever the license was given by this cruel and unnecessary rule. Captain Calhoun, mentions that while he and his companions were on their way to Richmond from North-eastern Georgia, where they were captured, they stopped at Atlanta, and just before they started, a sick soldier who was near the line, beyond which the prisoners were not allowed to go, put his hand over to pluck a bunch of leaves that were not a foot from the boundary. The instant he did so, the guard caught sight of him, fired, and killed him.

Another instance of equal skill in "shooting on the wing," will be noticed in the case of the soldier who only exposed his arm an instant in throwing out some water, and was wounded, fortunately not killed, by the rebel bullet. Something of the same kind was related in the course of conversation, but is not in the evidence, as happening at the Libby, when an officer was shot while waving his hand in farewell to a departing comrade.

But there were cruelties worse than these, because less the result of impulse and recklessness, and because deliberately done. There opens now a part of the narrative which is as amazing as it is unaccountable.

The reader will turn to the heart-rending scenes of famine which the testimony before the Commission has exposed.

The daily ration in the officers' quarter, of Libby prison, was a small loaf of bread about the size of a man's fist, made of Indian meal. Sometimes it was made from wheat flour, but of variable quality. It weighed a little over half a pound. With it was given a piece of beef weighing two ounces.

But it is not easy to describe this ration, it was so irregular in kind, quality and amount. Its general character is vividly indicated by a remark made in conversation, by one of the officers: "I would gladly," said he, with emphatic sincerity, "*gladly* have preferred the horse-feed in my father's stable."

During the summer and the early part of the fall, the ration seems to have been less insufficient, and less repulsive than it afterwards became. At no period was it enough to support life, at least in health, for a length of time, but however inadequate, it was not so to such a remarkable degree as to produce the evils which afterward ensued.

It was about the middle of last autumn that this process of slow starvation became intolerable, injurious, and cruel to the extent referred to. The corn bread began to be of the roughest and coarsest description. Portions of the cob and husk were often found ground in with the meal. The crust was so thick and hard that the prisoners called it iron-clad. To render the bread eatable, they grated it, and made mush of it, but the crust they could not grate.

Now and then, after long intervals, often of many weeks, a little meat was given them, perhaps two or three mouthfuls. At a later period, they received a pint of black peas, with some vinegar, every week. The peas were often full of worms, or maggots in a chrysalis state, which, when they made soup, floated on the surface.

Those who were entirely dependent on the prison fare, and who had no friends at the North to send them boxes of food, began to suffer the horrible agony of craving food, and feeling themselves day by day losing strength. Dreams and delusions began to distract their minds.*

Although many were relieved through the generosity of their more favored fellow prisoners, yet the supply from this source was, of course, inadequate. Captain Calhoun speaks of suffering "a burning sensation on the inside, with a general failing in strength." "I grew so foolish in my mind that I used to blame myself for not eating more when at home." "The subject of food engrossed my entire thoughts." "Captain Stevens having received a box from home, sat down and ate to excess, and died a few hours afterwards." "A man had a piece of ham which I looked at for hours, and would have stolen it I had had a chance."

One day, by pulling up a plank in the floor, they gained access to the cellar, and found there an abundance of provisions: barrels of the finest wheat flour, potatoes and turnips. Of these they ate ravenously until the theft was discovered.

But the most unaccountable and shameful act of all was yet to come. Shortly after this general diminution of rations, in the month of January last, the boxes, which before had been regularly delivered, and in good order, were withheld. No reason was given. Three hundred arrived every week, and were received by Colonel Ould, Commissioner of Exchange, but instead of being distributed, were retained, and piled up in warehouses near by, and in full sight of the tantalized and hungry captives. Three thousand were there when Lieutenant-Colonel Farnsworth came away.

There was some show of delivery, however, but in a manner especially heartless. Five or six of the boxes were given during the week. The eager prisoner, expectant perhaps of a wife's or mother's thoughtful provision for him, was called to the door and ordered to spread his blanket, when the open cans, whether containing preserved fruits, condensed milk, tobacco, vegetables, or meats, were thrown promiscuously together, and often ruined by the mingling.

These boxes sometimes contained clothing, as well as food, and their contents were frequently appropriated by the prison officials. Lieutenant McGinnis recognized his own home-suit of citizen's clothes on one of them, pointing out his name on the watch-pocket.

The officers were permitted to send out and buy articles at extravagant prices, and would find the clothes, stationery, hams and butter which they had purchased bearing the marks of the Sanitary Commission.

In one instance this constant thievery became an unexpected advantage to the inmates. After the famous "tunnelling out," by which so many effected their escape, the guards confessed that they had seen the fugitives, but supposed that they

---

* The very same phenomenon occurred during the celebrated Darien Exploring Expedition, under Lieutenant Strain, some years ago. The whole party suffered starvation; a number of them died, and the remainder were rescued when they had become emaciated and debilitated nearly to the point of death.

"From the time that food became scarce to the close, and just in proportion as famine increased, they revelled in gorgeous dinners. Truxton and Mauray would pass hours in spreading tables loaded with every luxury. Over this imaginary feast they would gloat with the pleasure of a gourmand." — *Darien Explor. Exped., Harpers' Monthly*, vol. x., p. 613.

The party separated, Strain and Avery being the least exhausted and going on before the others to obtain succor if possible.

"At length starvation produced the same singular effect on them that it did on Truxton and Mauray, and they would spend hours in describing all the good dinners they had ever eaten. For the last two or three days, when most reduced, Strain said that he occupied almost the whole time in arranging a magnificent dinner. Every luxury or curious dish that he had ever seen or heard of composed it, and he wore away the hours in going round his imaginary table, arranging and changing the several dishes. He could not force his mind from the contemplation of this, so wholly had one idea — food — taken possession of it." — *Darien Explor. Exped., Harp. Monthly*, vol. x., p. 750.

were their own men stealing the boxes! The tunnel, after running under the street, had its outlet near where the boxes were piled up.

All through the winter and late into the spring was this suffering, chiefly from hunger, prolonged. There is evidence of its continuation even so late as the month of May last.

Surgeon Ferguson, who was confined there at that time, gives a most painful picture of what he saw.

"No one can appreciate, without experience, the condition of the officers in the prison during the twelve days of my stay; their faces were pinched with hunger. I have seen an officer standing by the window, gnawing a bone like a dog. I asked him, 'What do you do it for?' His reply was, 'It will help fill up.'

"They were constantly complaining of hunger; there was a sad, and insatiable expression of face impossible to describe."

There is no suffering that can be mentioned greater than that of the slow and lingering pains of famine, except it be perhaps the agonies of absolute death from hunger — but of this no Libby evidence was collected. The description of Libby life might therefore end at this point so far as having reached the climax of all possible misery on the one hand, and of all possible barbarity on the other. But the testimony develops still other instances of cruelty, which may as well be introduced here, in order to show the animus of the Confederate authorities.

It is stated that for offences, whether trivial or serious, the prisoners were consigned to cells, beneath the prison, the walls of which were damp, green, and slimy. These apartments were never warmed, and often so crowded that some were obliged to stand up all night. It was in these dungeons that the hostages were placed.

But the inhumanity was not confined to the living. It extended even to the disposal of the dead. The bodies were placed in the cellar, to which the animals of the street had access, and very often were partly devoured by hogs, dogs, and rats. The officers had the curiosity to mark the coffins in which they were carried off, to find out whether they were buried in them. But they proved to be only vehicles for bearing them away, returning a score of times for others.

This must have been the case with privates only, who occupied part of the prison, as it is mentioned that the officers generally secured by contributions, made up among themselves, metallic coffins and a decent, temporary deposit in a vault for those of their number who died, until they could be removed to the North.

One other incident may be noticed which is quite in keeping with all the rest, but without the foregoing catalogue of outrages to humanity, would appear too shocking to be credible.

At the time Kilpatrick made his nearly successful raid on Richmond, the city was thrown into a panic by his approach, and the prison officials deliberately prepared — so the story runs — a more expeditious way of closing the career of their prisoners. It was somewhat more merciful than starvation, because it substituted instantaneous death for an endless agony of dying. The negroes gave the first intimation to the captives of what was going on.[*] Richard Turner took care to dash the hopes of his captives, as well as add to their anxiety by informing them that "Should Kilpatrick succeed in entering Richmond, it would not help them, as the prison authorities would blow up the prison, and all its inmates." Lieutenant Latouche was overheard observing to a rebel officer with whom he had entered the cellar, where the two hundred pounds of powder were said to be placed, "There is enough there to send every damned Yankee to Hell." Turner himself said, in the presence of Colonel Farnsworth, in answer to the question "Was the prison mined?" "Yes, and I would have blown you all to Hades before I would have suffered you to be rescued." The remark of Bishop Johns is corroborative as well as curious, in reply to the question, "Whether it was a Christian mode of warfare to blow up defenceless prisoners?" "I suppose the authorities are satisfied on that point, though I do not mean to justify it."

The idea is so monstrously shocking that the mind hesitates to grasp it, or believe it. Many will try to see in it only a menace to deter any further attempt to take Richmond by a raid. And yet the evidence, even if it does come by rebel admissions, has an air of diabolical sincerity. A remark of Turner's justifying the act, which was mentioned to one of the commissioners, but accidentally omitted in the formal testimony, gives quite a decided turn to the very natural probability that the fiendish plan was resolved upon: "Suppose Kilpatrick should have got in here, what would my life have been worth after you all got loose. Yes, I would have blown you all to Hades before I would have suffered you to be rescued." This was his argument and self-justification in brief, though somewhat more at length at the time.

The act was altogether consistent with the characters of the three men who had author-

[*] "Dug big hole down dar, massa. Torpedo in dar, sure!"

ity over the prison:— General Winder, the Commander of the Department, Major Turner, Commander of the Prison, whose brutality is fully illustrated by his management of it, and Richard Turner, Inspector of the Prison, by occupation a negro-whipper, (see the testimony of Colonel Farnsworth,) and whose savage nature vented itself in frequent acts of personal insult and physical violence toward the prisoners.

Be the story true or false, it is, at any rate, consummately befitting and consistent, inasmuch as the strongest reasons for its probability may be derived from the other facts that have now been narrated. If true, it is strongly corroborative of the vindictive purpose which animates the Confederate authorities. History may yet write it so, and therefore the Commissioners do not pass it over in silence because of any doubt that may cling to it.

Let the spectacle, that, probably, came so near taking place, be, at least, the appropriate crown and close of this portion of the narrative; the Union raiders, bounding over the fortifications of Richmond, intent upon rescuing their companions from a captivity worse than death,—and the three great brick buildings lifted bodily into the air, and let down in one stupendous crush and ruin upon the living forms of twelve hundred helpless men!

III.

Description of Belle Isle—No shelter provided from the heat in Summer, or from the cold in Winter—Sufferings during the late severe winter—Expedients to avoid Freezing to Death—Men Frozen to Death—The loathsome and inadequate Food—Men perishing from Hunger—Unavoidable Filth of the Camp and of the Men on account of the Rules—Neglect of the Sick—Cruelty to the Sick—Incidents of cruelty in Hospitals.

But there is a still lower depth of suffering to be exposed. The rank of the officers, however disregarded in most respects, induced some consideration, but for the private soldiers there seemed to be no regard whatever, and no sentiment which could restrain.

It is to this most melancholy part of their task that the Commissioners now proceed.

Belle Isle is a small island in the James river, opposite the Tredegar Iron-works, and in full sight from the Libby windows. It has pretensions enough to beauty at a distant view to justify its name, as part of it is a bluff covered with trees. But the portion on which the prisoners are confined, is low, sandy, and barren, without a tree to cast a shadow, and poured upon by the burning rays of a Southern sun.

Here is an enclosure, variously estimated to be from three to six acres in extent, surrounded by an earthwork about three feet high, with a ditch on either side. On the edge of the outer ditch, all round the enclosure, guards are stationed about forty feet apart, and keep watch there day and night. The interior has something of the look of an encampment, a number of Sibley tents being set in rows, with "streets" between. These tents, rotten, torn, full of holes,—poor shelter at any rate,—accommodated only a small proportion of the number who were confined within these low earth walls.

The number varied at different periods, but from ten to twelve thousand men have been imprisoned in this small space at one time, turned into the enclosure like so many cattle, to find what resting place they could. So crowded were they, that at the least, according to the estimated area given them, there could not have been but a space two feet by seven, and, at the most, three feet by nine, per man—hardly a generous allotment even for a "hospitable grave."

Some were so fortunate as to find shelter in the tents, but even they were often wet with the rain, and almost frozen when the winter set in. Every day some places were made vacant by disease or by death, as some were taken to the hospital, and some to burial.

But thousands had no tents, and no shelter of any kind. Nothing was provided for their accommodation. Lumber was plenty in a country of forests, but not a cabin or shed was built, although the commonest material would have been a grateful boon to the captives, and would have been quickly and ingeniously employed by them.

This is an established station for prisoners of war, and yet not a movement has been made, from its beginning to this moment, to erect barracks, or make any suitable and humane provisions for the comfort of those confined there. It remains to this day an open encampment, close under the walls of Richmond, and well known to the Confederate authorities, with nothing but the heavens for its canopy.

Here then these thousands lay all last summer, fall, and winter, with nought but the sand for their bed, and the sky for their covering. What did they do in the summer and early autumn, with the sickening heat of a torrid sun pouring upon their unprotected heads? What did they do when the rain descended and the floods came? What did they suffer when the malarious fog enveloped them, or when the sharp winds swept up the river, and pierced their almost naked and shivering forms.

Stripped of blankets and overcoats, hatless often, shoeless often, in ragged coats and rotting shirts, they were obliged to take the weather as it came. Here and there a tent had a fire, and the inmates gathered round it, but the thousands outside shivered as the cold cut them to the bone, and huddled together for warmth and sympathy.

The winter came—and one of the hardest winters ever experienced in the South—but still no better shelter was provided. The mercury was down to zero at Memphis, which is further south than Richmond. The snow lay deep on the ground around Richmond. The ice formed in the James, and flowed in masses upon the rapids, on either side of the island. Water, left in buckets on the island, froze two or three inches deep in a single night.

The men resorted to every expedient to keep from perishing. They lay in the ditch, as the most protected place, heaped upon one another, and lying close together, as one of them expressed it, "like hogs in winter," taking turns as to who should have the outside of the row. In the morning the row of the previous night was marked by the motionless forms of those "who were sleeping on in their last sleep"—*frozen to death!*

Every day, during the winter season, numbers were conveyed away stiff and stark, having fallen asleep in everlasting cold. Some of the men dug holes in the sand in which to take refuge. All through the night crowds of them were heard running up and down to keep themselves from freezing. And this fate threatened them, even more than it would have threatened most men, exposed to an equally severe temperature, even with such thin clothing and inadequate shelter—*for they were starving!*

The very sustenance of animal heat was withheld, and one of the most urgent occasions of hunger, a freezing temperature, which makes the bodily necessity stronger, and the appetite for food greater, was given full opportunity to make havoc among them. So the last stay and power of resistance was taken away—the cold froze them because they were hungry,—the hunger consumed them because they were cold. These two vultures fed upon their vitals, and no one in the Southern Confederacy had the mercy or the pity to drive them away. Only once was there heard a voice of indignant remonstrance in the rebel Congress from a noble-hearted statesman, but it was heard with indifference, and brought about no alleviation.

Read the rude words of these suffering men. Put together their testimony, and what a harrowing tale it tells!

They were fed as the swine are fed. A chunk of corn-bread, twelve or fourteen ounces in weight, half-baked, full of cracks as if baked in the sun, musty in taste, containing whole grains of corn, fragments of cob, and pieces of husks; meat often tainted, suspiciously like mule-meat, and a mere mouthful at that; two or three spoonfuls of rotten beans; soup thin and briny, often with the worms floating on the surface. None of these were given together, and the whole ration was never one-half the quantity necessary for the support of a healthy man.

The reader will not be surprised to hear that the men were ravenous when the rations were brought in, nor remain unmoved by the simple and touching expressions which fell from so many of them:—

"There was no name for our hunger."

"I was hungry—pretty nearly starved to death all the time."

"I waked up one night, and found myself gnawing my coat sleeve."

"I used to dream of having something good to eat."

"I walked the streets for many a night—I could not sleep for hunger."

"I lost flesh and strength, and so did the others, for want of food."

"If I were to sit here a week, I could not tell you half our suffering."

There were other indications of the desperate famine to which they were subjected. They gnawed the very bones which had been thrown away, sometimes breaking them up for soup. They were glad to get the refuse bread which was occasionally thrown to them by the guards. They even ate the rats which burrowed in the encampment. A dog, belonging to an officer, straying into the enclosure was caught and secreted, and before he could reclaim his property, it was torn apart by the man who stole it, some of it eaten by himself, and the remainder sold to his comrades.

So reduced were they, that they exchanged their clothing for food, and left themselves exposed the more to the cold. Under the temptation to secure double rations, many worked at their trades of blacksmithing and shoemaking for the rebel army.

But as the weary months drew on, hunger told its inevitable tale on them all. They grew weak and emaciated. Many found that they could not walk; when they attempted it a dizziness and blindness came, and they fell to the ground. Diarrhœa, scurvy, congestion of the lungs, and low fevers set in.

To add to their suffering there came the unavoidable consequences of being herded and crowded together, but in this case especially aggravated by a most unnecessary restriction. A broad beach surrounded the island, and yet only about seventy-five men were permitted to bathe per day in the river, in squads of five or six at a time. At this rate it was literally and almost accurately what so many of the men state: that they were allowed to wash themselves only once in six months.

"Lice were in all their quarters." Vermin and dirt encrusted their bodies. They were sore with lying in the sand. None, not even the sufferers with diarrhœa, were allowed to visit the sinks during the night, and in the morning the ground was covered and saturated with filth. The wells were tainted; the air was filled with disgusting odors.*

Many were taken sick daily, but were allowed to suffer for days before they were removed to the hospitals, and when this was done, it was often so late that the half of them died before reaching it, or died at the very moment their names were being recorded.

There was a hospital tent on the island, which was always full of the sick. It had no floor, the sick and dying were laid on straw, and logs were their only pillows. "If you or I saw a horse dying," said one, "wouldn't we put some straw under his head? Would we let him beat his head on a log in his agony?"

When this tent was full, the sick were taken to a hospital in Richmond.

The poor creatures were often as prematurely returned, as they had been tardily removed thither. Often were they seen escorted back, so weak as hardly to be able to move, some even crawling on their hands and knees. Colonel Ely, of the 18th Connecticut, saw one of his men, a former schoolmate and townsman, George Ward, a much respected citizen of Norwich, Connecticut, returning to the island in this condition, with a squad of others. He threw him a ham, but as the "poor fellow crawled to get it," says Colonel Farnsworth, who also witnessed the sad condition of an old acquaintance, "the rebel guard charged bayonets upon him, called him a damned Yankee, and appropriated the ham."

An incident which happened in the very hospital from which these men were brought will give even a better idea of how the sick were treated.

Two officers made their escape. Immediately all the patients who were able to sit up or stand were taken into an empty room under the Libby, and kept there twenty-four hours, without food or blankets, as a punishment for not having reported the contemplated escape. From this treatment Surgeon Pierce died. The officers in the room above took up the floor, supplied the sick with food and drink, and shared their blankets with them. For this they were deprived by Major Turner of rations for a whole day.

A still more vivid picture of a hospital interior is given by Surgeon Ferguson. It is of the notorious and horrible Hospital No. 21, where, so late as in May last, Dr. Ferguson says "the wounded Union prisoners were under treatment, * * * I consider," he adds, "the nourishment and stimulation they received entirely insufficient to give them a proper chance for recovery. I am surprised that more do not die. There were many bad cases among them that must inevitably sink under this treatment after a few days. The condition of these men was such, that any medical observer would impute it to insufficient stimulation and nutrition.

"The bedding where the privates were confined by wounds was very dirty; the covering was entirely old, dirty quilts; the beds were offensive from the discharges from wounds and secretions of the body, and were entirely unfit to place a sick or wounded man on.

"On the faces of the wounded was an anxious haggard expression of countenance, such as I have never seen before; I attribute it to want of care, want of nourishment and encouragement"

A Hospital Steward, while a prisoner, attending to some duty in the hospital, found, by accident, the Confederate Surgeon-General's quarterly report, which he brought away with him when he was paroled. By this, it appears that in the months of January, February and March last, out of nearly twenty-eight hundred patients, about fourteen hundred—or half the number—died! This document will be found in the appendix.*

And what was here done in prison and hospital, to our private soldiers on Belle Isle, and to our officers in the Libby, was done nearly all over the South. These facts are most conspicuous only because in the foreground. But from almost every station in the distant South, of which anything is known, comes the same story of robbery and insult, of starvation on food both bad and insufficient, of exposure—in the day to heat, and in the night to the frost—of shootings without warning, of close and filthy rooms or unsheltered encampments, of disease without care or medical treatment, and of deaths without number.

Danville has yet the whole of its dreadful tale to tell. Andersonville has yet to account for its average of one hundred and thirty deaths a day, at which rate the whole

---

* This taint of the drinking water was mentioned in conversation, but was accidentally omitted in the evidence.

* Page 55.

of its present number—thirty-five thousand—will be dead in a few months.*

The very railroads can speak of inhuman transportations from one point to another of the sick, the wounded, and the unwounded together, crowded into cattle and baggage cars, lying and dying in the filth of sickness, and the blood of undressed wounds.

IV.

The men as they appeared when brought on board the flag-of-truce boat, and into the Hospitals—Distressing spectacle—Hunger, nakedness, filthiness—Disease and death from starvation and cold—Cries for food—Imbecility and insanity of many—Opinions of the surgeons—The Medical Report of the Commission.

THE Commissioners do not feel at liberty, in presenting a narrative like this, every fact of which is rooted in the appended testimony, to make any inferential statements, although there are some incidents which are as essentially connected with such a state of things, as certain known effects are with certain established causes. A hundred scenes of suffering could be imagined and depicted by one conversant with the medical and other phenomena of famine and exposure to cold, which would be recognized as part of their own history by those who saw or experienced the wretched life led by the prisoners on Belle Isle.

But, as it has happened, the reader is furnished with vivid descriptions, by eye-witnesses, of the men as they appeared at the time of their transfer into the hands of the United States Government, and they have only to be imagined back on Belle Isle, or wherever else they had been, to get all too painful a conception of what was daily to be witnessed there.

"I have been," said Mr. Abbott, who, as special agent of the Sanitary Commission, was among the first to come in contact with the returned prisoners—" I have been on the battle-field, and in the hospitals, and witnessed much suffering, but never did I experience so sad and deplorable a condition of human beings as that of the paroled Union prisoners just from Belle Island, and the rebel prison of the South."

It was his business, for a period, to accompany the flag-of-truce boat as it plied between City Point, Virginia, and Annapolis, Maryland, bringing home thousands of the wretched men. The greater proportion of them were living skeletons, and each successive boat-load was in a worse condition than the last. Hundreds, at each trip, were stretched on cots, sick with every form of disease which could have been induced by confinement, exposure, and bad food. A number were dying; several died before the boat landed. Every one was in a frightfully filthy condition. All were deficient in clothing. Many were almost naked, and whatever they had on was ragged and dirty. Their hair and beards had grown long, having been uncut for many months. Their bodies were encrusted with dirt, and infested with vermin. One man had convulsions during a whole trip, caused, the surgeon said, by vermin. The vermin were very thick upon his body, and he threw his attenuated arms about, catching as at lice, throwing them off, and slapping them with his blanket.

In this state the prisoners were landed, and were received by the surgeons of Annapolis and Baltimore.

Many were so weak that they had to be carried ashore on stretchers, and died in the brief transit. Others tottered to the hospital, with the little strength they had remaining, only to die in a few hours. Some of them were found covered with bad and extensive sores, caused by lying on the sand. Many had lost their reason, and were in all stages of idiocy and imbecility.* One had become incurably insane in his joy at being delivered.

Often they acted like children and had to be taught again the decencies of life, so long had they been unhabituated to them. A number had partially lost their sight, hearing, and speech. One man was pointed out to the commissioners who had been so covered by vermin, that after having been, as was supposed, thoroughly washed, his head even been shaven, was laid upon a

---

* At the very moment this inquiry is concluded and this report is being prepared, a memorial is brought to the President of the United States by commissioners appointed by the prisoners still in confinement at Andersonville, representing their sufferings and appealing for succor. A statement is also published, verified under oath by three of these soldiers, who were exchanged August 16th. These documents are so remarkably corroborative, in every particular, of the results developed by the inquiry, and, in some respects, represent a state of things so much worse than at the date at which the investigation closed, that they have been appended in a supplement, which will be found, after the evidence, on page 259. The frequent menacing predictions of the rebel press, and the evident precipitation of cruel measures upon the prisoners which is exhibited by the testimony taken before the Commission, find a fitting confirmation and counterpart, in this the latest account which has come from a Southern prison.

* "Wilson was exceedingly debilitated, and had become perfectly childish, and almost idiotic from suffering, and Strain feared that bad effects might ensue if he was permitted to eat as much as he wished." *Darien Explor. Exped. Harpers Month.* vol. x. p. 752.

clean bed—in ten minutes the sheets and his clothing were covered with vermin again. And this was not peculiar to him. It was only an instance of the unavoidable condition of all. In some cases they were so eaten by lice as to very nearly resemble a case of scabbing from small pox, being covered with sores from head to foot.

Many had been badly frost-bitten, and came ashore with feet partially amputated. In one case it was mentioned to the visitors that a frozen foot fell off as the man was being carried ashore!

Without exception they were ravenous for food. Their cries for something to eat were pitiful to hear. The surgeons had to restrain their voracity, and keep them on small quantities of liquid food lest they should kill themselves by over-eating or by eating solid food. They would often entreat for the sight of an apple or a piece of meat, that they might enjoy at least the vision of what they could not have.

It was their invariable reply in answer to the question, "What was the matter?" "That they had been starved, exposed, and neglected on Belle Isle?"

The surgeons, themselves, were unanimous in their opinion as to the cause of their condition, not only from the uniform story of the men, but from the characteristics of the different diseases, the revelations of the post-mortem examination, and especially, and most conclusively of all, the invariable treatment which proved most efficacious; namely, not medication, but simple nutrition and stimulation.

They all agreed in attributing the condition of the men to one or more of the following causes: Deprivation of clothing; insufficient food, in quantity and quality; want of fresh air on account of over-crowding; consequent and unavoidable uncleanliness; want of adequate shelter during the fall and winter; and mental depression the natural result of all.

The reader will be impressed by the emphatic utterances of the surgeons:

SURGEON VANDERKIEFT.—"Their condition is on account of ill-treatment by starvation and exposure, as I am convinced is the case by their actual condition on their arrival, and by rations shown to me. That the men must have been in good health when captured, I do not need such a statement, as I am well acquainted with the regulations which govern the medical department of our army, 'to send to the rear every man who is not perfectly able to bear arms.' * * *

"The diseases most common among these returned prisoners are scurvy, diarrhœa, and congestion of the lungs, which are not amenable to the ordinary treatment in use in civil life, or in hospitals of our own army; they are most successfully mastered by high nutrition and stimulation, with cleanliness and fresh air—medicinal treatment being of small assistance in the recovery of the sufferers, and often being entirely dispensed with, * * * thus proving by the counteracting effect of good food, air, cleanliness, and stimulants, that these disorders are the result of the causes above stated."

SURGEON ELY.—Speaking of the dead whom he had found on the boats as they landed, "No words can describe their appearance. In each case the sunken eye, the gaping mouth, the filthy skin, the clothes and head alive with vermin, the repelling bony contour, all conspired to lead to the conclusion that we were looking upon the victims of starvation, cruelty, and exposure, to a degree unparalleled in the history of humanity. Nearly every instance leads us irresistibly to the conclusion that death has been owing to a long series of exposures and hardships, with a deprivation of the barest necessities of existence. * * * *

"In many cases that I have observed, the dirt incrustation has been so thick as to require *months* of constant ablutions to recover the normal condition and function of the integuments. Patients have repeatedly stated in answer to my interrogatories that they had been unable to wash their bodies once in six months, that all that time they had lain in the dirt. * * * In many instances this is the prime, exciting cause of the diseases of the pulmonary and abdominal organs which are so constantly found among our Richmond patients." *

SURGEON PARKER.—" The majority of the diseased cases were diarrhœa, caused by bad diet, of insufficient and bad quality. They have resulted from the want of variety of diet. I found nutrition was the most successful treatment. I do not consider the (rebel) rations, I have seen, sufficient for the support of life for any long time."

SURGEON PETERS.—" The post-mortems have made apparent diseases of nearly all the viscera to a remarkable extent.† Under a spare but concentrated diet many have rallied. In one instance a boy gained fifty pounds in two weeks. I think nine-tenths of the men weighed under one hundred pounds. They had an uncontrollable appetite."

SURGEON CHAPEL.—" We were obliged

---

* See his evidence for a report at length of the results of the post-mortem examinations. Appendix p. 48.

† See Dr. Carpenter on Starvation, where fifty-two per cent of the starved were thus affected.

to treat them as children in regulating their diet, having to restrain their over-eating, and confine them to a concentrated, but nourishing and generous diet. Several cases had no disease whatever, but suffered from extreme emaciation and starvation * * * * All gave evidence of extensive visceral disease, of which starvation, cold and neglect were undoubtedly the primary cause. Some of the cases sank from extreme debility, without any evidence of disease as the cause of death."

The professional opinions of these gentlemen, and the other incidental medical testimony scattered through the appendix, will, without doubt, be received with great weight by the reader. But, after all, the evidence of the men themselves, rudely and abruptly worded, and so often unconsciously graphic and pathetic, will come more convincingly to the popular heart.

It will be enough for most people that the captives were *hungry* day and night, and suffered the gnawing pains of famine, with its dreams and delusions. It will be enough that they became weak and emaciated to the degree in which they were found when exchanged. It will be enough that they were poisoned by foul air and over-crowding; and that they were exposed in the depth of winter to the cold, without shelter and without covering. It will be enough that thousands of them became hideously diseased, and that most of them miserably perished.

People do not need any other information in the face of such facts as these in order to come to a just conclusion, and yet there is a certainty and a satisfaction in scientific facts, and in the testimony of nature, which ought to be recognized in an investigation like this.

For this reason the commissioners made the investigation also a scientific one, and append a medical statement, prepared at their request by one of their number, drawn likewise from the evidence, the facts and arguments of which are fully indorsed by the medical members of the commission.

V.

Reported suffering of the Rebel Army, and Embarrassment of the Rebel Government for want of Supplies, as an Excuse for Denying Food and Clothing to United States Soldiers—The Imposibility of there being any such Deficiency—The Physical Condition of the Rebel Army perfect—Facts drawn from Rebel testimony.

It has been said, and has been the general impression, that the rebel government was itself embarrassed for want of supplies—that its own soldiers were naked and hungry, and that even the prison guards shared the privations of the prisoners.

It will be noticed that this excuse, urged strenuously by their friends, and half accepted by every one disposed to be moderate and just, after all, only accounts for a small portion of the conduct of the rebels to their captives.

Why were they robbed of their private property: the money, and the few trinkets a man usually carries with him? Or, if this was the uncontrollable habit of a wild soldiery, why was it the regular proceeding of the Libby authorities on the entrance of an officer? Why was it often done with brutal violence, when the person undergoing the process expostulated?

By whose connivance were the supplies of food and clothing, sent from the North, stolen? By whose neglect, or by whose order, were they withheld in immense quantities from men palpably starving and freezing?

How is it that—after three years of war, during which everything military had grown colossal and correspondingly complete, with them, as with us,—that no extensive barracks, even of the cheapest and frailest kind, offering, at least, space to move in, and shelter from the weather, were not erected; but that open encampments, or city warehouses too small for such occupation, continue in use to this day?

How is it that, even under such circumstances, supposing them, for some reason, unable to have done better, they made rules circumscribing the prisoners still further, exposing them to the poison of foul air, generated by unavoidable personal uncleanliness, and by the equally unavoidable accumulations of filth under certain conditions of disease, for which either no provision was made, or if made, they were capriciously prevented from using? *

Why, when over-crowding a building with captives, did they make an imaginary boundary line, two or three feet inside the windows, to be observed under penalty of instant death? How is it that the guards were not only permitted, by this regulation, to amuse themselves with taking the lives of the prisoners, upon certain given opportunities, but were negatively encouraged even to murder and assassination, by the indifference of the prison authorities?

* "Sometimes we were allowed to go to the privy, and sometimes we were not. We have been kept from it so much as three days, until we fouled the floor." Appendix, page 24.

"After we tunnelled out, we were only allowed to go to the privy six at a time; the floor was in one mess—filthy; an ordinary one horse wagon load of human excrement on the floor every morning." Appendix, page 39.

"The enclosure on Belle Isle was a mass of filth every morning, from the inability of the men to proceed to the sinks after evening." Appendix.

And is there anything to account for the condition of their hospitals for prisoners? Even supposing them to be ill-supplied with medicines, there were common remedies, easily at hand, which were seldom administered—or supposing them to be ill-furnished with hospital comforts, even with sheets and bedding, there was no necessity for placing the *wounded*, as well as the sick, on beds too foul to approach, and afterward made still more offensive by the permitted accumulations of the secretions and putrid discharges of the patients.

Why, also, when their arrangements induced so much sickness and disease, did they leave the men to suffer, often for weeks, before they removed them (and then like sick animals) from the encampment or the prison to the hospital, often to die on the way, or as soon as they were put in the hands of a physician? Why did they discharge them when so feeble that they reeled back to the place of captivity, and even had to crawl thither on their hands and knees? Or why, as in one instance (and one, under such circumstances, may be many), did they subject them, even before they were convalescent and discharged, to such a punishment as confinement in a cell, exposure to cold, and deprivation of food?

These grave developments of the testimony, by no means new to many at the North, and occasionally the subject of newspaper report (though never in such detail as now related), have as yet elicited no excuse or explanation; and until an excuse or explanation comes, the government by whom such things are authorized, and the people by whose public sentiment such things are encouraged, will stand arraigned for almost immeasurable inhumanity and criminality before the civilized world.

But it is important that this matter of famine and freezing, suffered by our men, should take more than a negative place among the foregoing positive facts, as half explained away, if it should appear that neither were necessary or unavoidable.

These are the two worst developments of the inquiry—the facts cannot be denied, for no evidence was ever more closely knit in support of anything, and the question, therefore, lies open: Were the people who were capable of these other unaccountable and inexcusable acts, capable, also, of deliberately withholding necessary food from their prisoners of war, and furnishing them with what was indigestible and loathsome, when their own army was abundantly supplied with good and wholesome food? Were they capable, also, not only of depriving their prisoners of their own clothing, but also of withholding the issue of sufficient to keep them warm, when the soldiers of their own army were well-equipped, and well-protected from exposure to the wet and cold?

But the inquiry cannot stop at this point. If they were capable of this, then they were capable of beholding, without compassion, their fellow beings subjected to the worst and most lingering agonies which humanity can endure. Putting together the act, and this insensibility to its consequences, what other deduction can be drawn, than that all was a pre-determined plan, originating somewhere in the rebel counsels, for destroying and disabling the soldiers of their enemy, who had honorably surrendered in the field?

And has it come to this? Has the oft-threatened black flag, the signal of a foe that has no mercy and gives no quarter, been floating all this time, not courageously on the battle field, but over prisons and hospitals in the South, full of surrendered and helpless men?

The commissioners, from the outset, considered this department of their investigation to be fully as important as the other, and were at equal pains to leave it no longer a matter of doubt whether or not the rebel government was unable to provide their prisoners with food and clothing, good and sufficient.

One fact was evident on the face of things, that no army could have endured such forced and violent marches, the fatigues and exposures of such desperate campaigning, and have kept up a spirit for such indomitable fighting, unless they had been well-equipped, and their physical condition had been maintained by every means, medical and commissary, known in a well regulated army.

The rebel authorities could not afford to swell their army by conscription on the one hand, and to let the material, thus obtained, escape its military use, by famine and disease on the other. The same arbitrary energy which could enforce the one, could provide against the other.

Nor are the quotations of Confederate prices any criterion by which to judge. The country is rich and fertile, if the Confederate currency is inflated and poor. Every agricultural resource of a soil and climate, unsurpassed by any other in the world, has been quickened to meet the emergency. The necessity has, also, in three years, developed other and unknown fountains of supply—all at the command of a strong, desperate, and despotic government, which has not hesitated to employ every means to keep its armies on the most perfect military footing.

This reasoning is borne out by the facts developed in the inquiry. The testimony will be found to be quite a revelation of the rebel mode of sustaining an army and a war. Their efficiency in this respect must be admitted—an efficiency created partly by a greater aptitude and inclination for the single art of war, than for the many arts of peace; and partly by the deadly necessity they are under for the most strenuous possible defence of their rebellion, on account of the extraordinary power developed by the Government of the United States.

It appears, from the testimony, that the guards of the prisoners (of whose privations so much has been said) were better supplied with food than the prisoners. The question was frequently asked, and elicited the invariable reply, that they did not share the same ration. Their supply was of a different character, and was enough. Sometimes they threw fragments of food to the hungry captives on Belle Isle. It will be remembered, that at the time the Libby prisoners were so insufficiently fed, a room in the cellar was found stocked with provisions of excellent quality.

But no testimony on this point can be so satisfactory as that derived from the rebel soldiers themselves.

Several of the commissioners went directly from Annapolis to Washington for the express purpose of visiting and examining the rebel prisoners. They found a large number at the Lincoln Hospital. Although these prisoners were suffering from wounds received in the late battles of the Wilderness and Spottsylvania, they were in a physical condition which alone was evidence enough of the care that had been taken of them by their own government. In every case they were healthy, hardy, vigorous men. There was scarcely a trace even of the terrible fatigue they had so recently endured. Better than all, as an indication of their condition, their wounds were healing as only the wounds of men in perfect health can heal.

Nine, out of the whole number, were examined under oath. The formal testimony stopped at this number, as it was found by conversation, that all had the same account to give, and it was needless to multiply depositions. They came from six of the principal States of the Confederacy. Two were from Virginia, two from South Carolina, two from Georgia, one from Mississippi, one from North Carolina, and one from Alabama.

In order to make the inquiry more complete and satisfactory, certain members of the Commission afterwards visited Fort Delaware, and the Hospital on David's Island, New York, at both which stations rebels were confined, and the testimony of eleven more was procured. The men were from Virginia, Georgia, North Carolina and Mississippi.

The evidence of these three separate sets of witnesses, which has been placed together, was given without hesitation, and is uniform and reliable. Any amount of such could have been procured, but that which has been taken will be found full enough.

The result of the whole amounts to this: In the words of one of them—"They had nothing to complain of in the way of food and clothing." They were supplied with rations, only a few ounces less than the overgenerous ration of the United States army.

The quality of the rebel ration was as satisfactory to the rebels as the quantity. The corn-bread was excellent, made by themselves from fine meal. One of them naively observed that he preferred it to Northern meal! They had never had any meal furnished them of that quality which was ground with the cobs and husks, and in which whole grains of corn occasionally appeared. This inferior kind, they said, was "given to stock."

The only time in which they suffered any privation was on a forced march, when they were in advance of their supplies—a matter liable to occur in any army.

In winter they lived in cabins or tents, well warmed, and well supplied with fuel. None ever suffered from the cold. In summer they were sheltered by tents, but these they left behind when on a campaign. They were fully supplied with clothing and with blankets or oilcloths. A requisition on the quartermaster could always procure any article that was necessary. When engaged in active service, however, they carried as little as possible, only the clothes they had on and a single blanket, but no man was restricted as to the amount he might carry. It may be imagined what a condition they were in, under this system, as respects dirt, vermin, and rags, after a long campaign and a pitched battle.

They describe the hospitals, both in the city and in the field, as comfortable, and with sufficient medical attendance. The bedding and sheets in Hospital No. 4, in Richmond, was said by one of them to be fully as good as those on David's Island, New York. There were also the usual delicacies for the sick.

From all this, it appears that the Southern army has been, ever since its organization, completely equipped in all necessary respects, and that the men have been supplied with everything which would keep them in the best condition of mind and body, for the hard and desperate service in which they were engaged. They knew nothing of famine or freezing. Their wounded and sick were never neglected.

So do the few details of fact that could be

extracted, without suspicion of their object, from the soldiers of the Southern army, confirm the reasoning which accounts for its efficiency.

The conclusion is inevitable. It was in their power to feed sufficiently, and to clothe, whenever necessary, their prisoners of war. They were perfectly able to include them in their military establishment; but they chose to exclude them from the position always assigned to such, and in no respect to treat them like men taken in honorable warfare. Their commonest soldier was never compelled, by hunger, to eat the disgusting rations furnished at the Libby to United States officers. Their most exposed encampment, however temporary, never beheld the scenes of suffering which occurred daily and nightly among United States soldiers in the encampment on Belle Isle.

The excuse and explanation are swept away. There is nothing now between the Northern people and the dreadful reality.

VI.

The treatment of rebel prisoners at United States Stations—The humane orders of the Government—Scene at Lincoln Hospital—Interior of the Station at Fort Delaware—The Hospital on David's Island—Johnson's Island—Point Lookout—Tender care of sick and wounded Rebels at all these Stations—Kind treatment of the wounded prisoners—Abundant shelter, fuel, clothing, and food furnished them—Facilities for bathing and exercise—Small mortality—No robbing—No shooting—No abuse—Christian burial of the dead—The contrast of the Union and Rebel prisoners at the moment of exchange.

THE moment has now come for the reverse to this melancholy picture, and it will be as grateful to the American people at large, as it was to the Commissioners.

Early in the progress of their investigation, while in the midst of the sufferers taking their testimony, and occasionally hearing floating and irresponsible rumors of equal neglect and cruelty on our part toward the rebel prisoners in our hands, they determined to make a full inquiry into the conduct and management of United States Stations where they were confined.

A large proportion of the testimony will be found devoted to this department. The variety and the widely separate sources of the evidence, will only make more conspicuous its absolute unity and truth. It reveals an impressive contrast, point for point, with that which has just been narrated, and has turned out to be entirely confirmatory of what Quartermaster-General Meigs declares in his letter,* "that such prisoners are treated with all the consideration and kindness that might be expected of a humane and Christian people."

The design of the Government is fully exhibited in the circular orders issued by Colonel Hoffman, Commissary-General of Prisoners.†

The ration was to be generous and abundant; its elements of the fullest variety. The amount issued being greater than a man could consume, the excess over that which was given, was to go to the formation of a Prison fund, which was to be applied in various ways, (not expressly provided for in the army regulations,) that would promote the health and comfort of the prisoners.

Army clothing was to be furnished by requisition, whenever needed, the only difference being that the buttons and trimmings were to be taken from the coats, and the skirts cut so short that the captives should not be mistaken for United States soldiers.

Careful accounts were to be kept of the money and valuables taken from each prisoner, which accounts were to accompany him, if transferred from one post to another; and when paroled, the articles were to be returned. They were to be permitted to correspond with their friends. All articles that were sent to them were to be delivered, if not contraband.

The hospital had its separate provisions. The keepers in charge were to be "responsible to the commanding officer for its good order, *and the proper treatment of the sick.*" A fund for each hospital was to be created, as in other United States hospitals, and to be expended for the comfort of the sick, and "objects indispensably necessary to promote the sanitary condition of the hospital."

The minute directions of the entire order look equally to the security of the prisoners, and to all that is necessary for them in health or sickness.

The commissioners are able to testify that the order is fully carried out. They took pains not only to procure evidence as to the fact, but to see for themselves.

Two members of the Commission came, without previous notice, to the Lincoln hospital in Washington, where they had heard that several hundred of the rebels lay having been wounded in the recent battles. The chief object of the visitors at the time has been already mentioned. But they were able also to observe how well the hospital was conducted.

Although arriving at an unseasonable

* See page 55.
† The whole document will be found on page 56.

hour, when the surgeons and nurses were examining and dressing the wounds, they were instantly admitted, with marked and cordial courtesy, by Chief Surgeon McKee, upon his learning the mission upon which they had come.

The wards were airy and neat, free from offensive odor, the beds so clean that the visitors sat upon them while taking testimony. The men themselves were cheerful and good-natured, the more slightly wounded crowding up curiously to know what was going on, until requested to retire. Some were sitting by their beds reading novels or odd numbers of periodicals, now and then a bible. They were always ready to converse, and answered the questions that were put to them without hesitation.

The visitors could see no difference in these two wards from the twenty or more others in the same hospital that were appropriated to the United States soldiers. The patients were mostly in clean, white underclothing, and if it had not been for a figure in butternut-colored uniform here and there, nothing would have suggested the presence of an enemy.

The wounds were being tenderly unbandaged and dressed by the surgeons and their assistants. Kindness and attention were visible everywhere. Female nurses and a white-hooded Sister of Charity were constantly moving from bed to bed. One of them was seen carrying a waiter of iced porter to the wounded, and holding the glass to the lips of the more helpless.

The spectacle was in remarkable contrast with that which had been described by Dr. Ferguson, only the evening before, as witnessed by him in Hospital No. 21, Richmond, where our soldiers lay amid the secretions of their body, and the purulent discharges of their wounds, dying of neglect, and for want of the commonest medical attention.

Some time after this, two members of the commission made an especial visit to Fort Delaware, for the express purpose of examining into the prison and hospital arrangements there, in order to give, in this narrative, their own direct testimony and description, as well as whatever evidence they might be able to collect.

They fixed upon Fort Delaware because it was one of the most extensive of the United States stations for prisoners of war, and because it had been the object of various rebel reports.*

The following description is from notes taken on the spot by one of the party, and written out immediately afterward:

"The prisoners numbering between eight and nine thousand were lodged outside the walls of the fort, (which is situated on an island,) in well built and ventilated barracks, and have free access at all hours to the adjoining enclosures for air and exercise. They were permitted, and, indeed, urged to bathe in squads in the river and to wash in sluices to which the tide had access twice in the twenty-four hours, and the facilities for these purposes were so great that any man might, if he chose, wash his whole person every day, and swim in the Delaware twice a week.

"Every man is furnished with a commodious bunk, with the head raised at a proper inclination above the feet, presenting a striking contrast to a Confederate prison, where prisoners sleep on the floor, or on the earth, and have not even a bunch of straw between them and the ground.

"The result of these precautions, and of the superior ventilation of the barracks was to render the quarters of the prisoners free from the unpleasant odor which generally exists where large number of men are brought together, and compelled to live in common. The same remark applies to the hospitals, which are spacious, clean, and in good order.

"When we went through the barracks, shortly before sunset, the men were generally out of doors walking about, talking, playing cards, washing, or occupying themselves in other ways. They appeared in general, contented and cheerful. Many of them had improvised sutler's shops, and were seated on the ground or boxes, selling coffee, broiled ham, bread, and other articles of food to their comrades, who were gathered around laughing and chatting.

"The means to prosecute this traffic came, we were told, from sympathizing friends in different parts of the Union, and from small sums of money paid as wages to such of the men as were willing to be detailed to perform various duties outside of the barracks at different points on the island. We tasted the coffee, which was sold for five cents a pint, and found it well made and palatable.

"Much good humor seemed to prevail, and there was not a little good-natured laughter while we were making the purchase. We were struck by the assured yet affable air with which General Schöpf moved through

---

* A recent specimen from the *Richmond Despatch*, July 14th. Speaking of some returned prisoners, the account runs: "They were subsequently imprisoned at Fort Delaware, where those who had money fared pretty well, but others, less fortunate, suffered many privations.

They state, that the condition of the Confederate prisoners at that point is deplorable in the extreme, and strongly urge the adoption of some measures for their relief. Sickness is very prevalent among them, while the rations are meagre and of poor quality."

the dense throng that pressed to look at the visitors. He was unattended even by an orderly His manner indicated a consciousness that he had nothing to fear from individual resentment.

"In addition to the water of the river which, as already stated, is accessible at all times for the purposes of cleanliness, thirty thousand gallons of drinking water are brought every day from the Brandywine, and distributed among the prisoners and the soldiers of the garrison, by means of large hose and a forcing pump worked by a steam engine. Health and comfort are therefore studied in this as in other particulars, but it was at first found difficult to prevent the prisoners from drinking from shallow wells dug by themselves, the water of which is brackish, and has a tendency to produce disease.

"The rations issued to the prisoners were the subject of an attentive examination. We tasted the bread, which is made of four parts of flour and one of Indian meal, and found it of superior quality, sweet and palatable; better indeed than is met with at hotels or places of resort in the country; quite as good as may be found in any well-ordered family. The meat was also sweet and of good quality. The diet is judiciously varied, potatoes and fresh vegetables being furnished in large quantities, wherever the health of the men appears to require it. The rations actually received by the prisoners until the 1st of June, 1864, were nearly three pounds of solid food for each man per day, besides coffee, sugar, molasses, etc. The quantity was then reduced to about thirty-four and a half ounces per diem.*

"The health of the prisoners is as carefully considered in the matter of clothing, as in other respects; those who require blankets or additional garments being supplied with them on proper application. Large numbers of coats, pantaloons, etc., were issued in this way during the past and previous winters. When a prisoner is placed on the sick list, and taken to the hospital, he is put in a warm bath, supplied with clean under-clothing, and then laid on a bed with clean sheets, in an airy apartment, where his condition is, so far as his disease will permit, one not only of comparative but absolute comfort.

"The percentage of deaths at Fort Delaware was, during some months of last autumn and winter, large. This result arose from a variety of causes originating before the prisoners were captured and brought to the island, and which the officers there could not at first remove or control. Among these may be enumerated the want of vaccination, which seems to be as rare among the poorer classes of the South as it is general at the North; the attempts made by the prisoners to vaccinate each other, which often caused disease of a dangerous type from the character of the virus employed; and the bad state of the body of many of the men taken at and near Vicksburg, who were broken down by hardships and fatigues sustained before their capture, as well as by the influence of the terrible malaria of the South.

"But while the ratio of mortality among the American soldiers in the hands of the rebels has continued to augment with time, the health of the Confederate prisoners at Fort Delaware has, on the contrary, improved under the influence of good food or kind treatment, until in May, 1864, but sixty-two died out of eight thousand one hundred and twenty-six confined at the island.

"The cruel and unusual rule by which an approach to the windows from inadvertence, or for the most innocent purpose, is made an offense punishable with death in the Confederate prisons, is, it need hardly be said, unknown in Fort Delaware. Few restraints are imposed, and those only such as are imperatively necessary for the preservation of order and cleanliness among a numerous and motley crowd, which necessarily contains some men of gross and filthy habits." *

Shooting was never resorted to unless a rule was grossly and persistently violated. Even then the direction was to order the prisoner "three distinct times to halt;" and if he "failed to halt, when so ordered, the sentinel must enforce his order by bayonet or ball." There were but five instances of shooting, under these instructions, and they were in every case in obedience to them.

It is hardly worth while to notice the question whether any were shot for looking out of the windows. No such order was ever given in this, or any other United States Station. Here the windows were seen filled with the prisoners.

The Commissioners are under great obligations to General Schöpf, Commander of the Post, for the courtesy shown them, in personally conducting them over the station, and to the surgeons and officers in attendance, who readily furnished all the evidence that was asked for. It was here that the documents, the general circular, the orders, and the schedules of rations and clothing were obtained.

* From notes by Judge Hare.

---

* "The reduction recently made in the prisoner's rations," writes Quartermaster-General Meigs, June 6th, "was for the purpose of bringing it nearer to what the rebel authorities profess to allow their soldiers, and no complaint has been heard of its insufficiency."

The testimony is exceedingly full and satisfactory on all points. It will be noticed that a prison fund was formed, in accordance with the regulations, from the excess of the ration *issued* over the ration *given*, and that the amount was spent for vegetables, and articles of convenience. But even with this withholding of part, so great was the abundance of food, that the prisoners hid loaves of bread, crackers and meat under the bunks. These were repeatedly found there in large quantities during an examination of the barracks.

Capt. Clark was able to save sometimes between two and three thousand dollars a month out of surplus rations, and yet every care was taken that too much was not withheld. The overseers were frequently asked if the prisoners complained of not having enough, and were ordered "to give them more, and let no man want." A complaint was scarcely ever heard.

It will be noticed what enormous quantities of clothing were issued, at this post alone, to the prisoners. In eight months over thirty-five thousand articles were distributed, comprising every species of clothing from shoes and stockings, shirts and drawers, to woollen blankets and great coats. Most of these were given on the approach of cold weather.

Every one without a blanket or overcoat of his own was provided with one. All had at least two blankets, and those who were delicate had more.

The barracks were made comfortable by stoves. Fuel was never wanting, and the fires were kept up by attendants. No less than thirteen hundred tons of coal were consumed last winter and spring by the prisoners.

In hot weather equal provision was made for their comfort, especially in the hospitals. The visitors noticed in the latter, even green shades covering the windows, and a water-cooler in every ward, filled with ice, for the free use of the patients.

Gen. Schöpf informed the visitors that in every case of death, the body was removed to a neat grave yard on the opposite shore, and the burial service of the Episcopal church was read over the grave.

It was found, by further investigation, that the arrangements of every other United States Prison Station and Hospital were the same as those of Fort Delaware. The same regulations were observed in all. The identical diet-table, containing the minute directions of the Surgeon-General at Washington, was hung up as conspicuously in the hospital for rebels as that for the United States soldier.

The De Camp General Hospital, on David's Island, New York, was a counterpart of that just described. The testimony taken by one of the commissioners, is almost a repetition of that taken at Fort Delaware. The only variations which occur are additions to the facts already recited.

None of the prisoners were ever deprived of money or valuables. Some of them had arrived in a filthy, horrible condition, ragged, barefooted and bareheaded, covered with vermin, (a condition easily accounted for by the peculiar and desperate style of Southern campaigning, where no tents or baggage were allowed to encumber, and the soldier had to wear the same unchanged suit through many days of forced marching and violent fighting.) Within a few hours the men, having been stripped of all their clothing, which was removed and burned, were washed, furnished with clean linen, and placed on clean, well-aired beds. Full suits of clothing were issued to them. When the weather became cold they were removed from tents to spacious pavilions, furnished with abundant fuel. No one was ever frostbitten. None were ever shot at. They were given the whole island inside the line of sentries for exercise. Formerly they had been allowed to go fishing and clamming, till several escaped, when the line of sentries was placed on the beach.

They had precisely the same rations as the Federal sick and wounded. Drinking water, cooled with ice, was furnished in profusion. Soap, towels, and combs were distributed for their private use. There was a nurse to every ten of them.*

It will not surprise the reader to hear of the small mortality, although nine-tenths were suffering from wounds.

One most pleasing feature of this hospital is developed in the testimony of Rev. Mr. Lowry, its chaplain. A library of two thousand volumes, formerly used by the United States soldiers, was even more used by the Confederates. They were furnished with Bibles, Prayer Books, and other religious publications. Religious services were held twice on Sunday, and two or three times during the week. The chapel, which would accommodate three hundred, was often crowded. Whenever a death occurred, the funeral was conducted according to the form of the Episcopal church.

Johnson's Island, in Ohio, has been an especial subject of rebel mis-statements. It is a pleasant, healthy spot, three hundred acres in extent, in Sandusky Bay, close in the neighborhood of Kelley's Island, which is a

* Each pavilion had from two to four water closets. Chairs and bed pans were provided for those unable to reach them. Ample structures were also erected on the beach.

favorite place of summer resort. The two Islands are much alike.

The climate is testified to be as favorable to health as that of Newport or Saratoga in summer, or Cincinnati and Dayton in winter. Like Fort Delaware it is a military prison and hospital. The buildings are spacious, new, and in good order. The sanitary and other regulations of similar stations are observed here in all particulars.

Although in winter the weather was so cold that the lake was frozen to the main land, three miles distant, and the government teams, conveying supplies, were able to cross upon the ice, yet so well warmed were the barracks, that not a single instance of treatment for exposure to cold was known, except in the case of some who attempted to escape.

A spacious square, enclosed by the buildings, was given up to the prisoners for exercise, and they were allowed to be in the open air all day.

The statistics of mortality will be astonishing to read, after hearing the rebel stories. In twenty-one months, out of an aggregate of six thousand four hundred and ten prisoners, there were only one hundred and thirty-four deaths. The number in prison at one time never exceeded two thousand seven hundred. In the months of May and June last, there were about two thousand three hundred prisoners. In May five died; in June only one!

Point Lookout was still another post which had been subjected to the rebel statement that the prisoners there suffered from cruelty and neglect. Miss Dix, who visited those very prisoners, sufficiently disposes of the slander. She says, "They were supplied with vegetables, with the best wheat bread, and fresh and salt meat three times daily in abundant measure — the full government ration.

"In the camp of about nine thousand rebel prisoners, there were but four hundred reported to the surgeon. Of these one hundred were confined to their beds, thirty were very sick, and perhaps fifteen or twenty would never recover.

"The hospital food consisted of beef-tea, beef-soup, rice, milk-punch, milk, gruel, lemonade, stewed fruits, beefsteak, vegetables, and mutton. White sugar was employed in cooking. The supplies were, in fact, more ample and abundant than in hospitals where our own men were under treatment."

The surgeons of the various hospitals, in several instances, allude to the excellent condition of the prisoners when discharged and exchanged, and in the statement of Miss Dix will be found a brief description of their appearance when leaving the flag-of-truce boat for their own lines: "All were in vigorous health, equipped in clothes furnished by the United States Government, many of them with blankets and haversacks."

And here terminates the contrast, which the reader has probably been drawing throughout, between the military stations for prisoners, North and South, Union and Rebel.

But the contrast must have been overwhelming at the point to which this narrative has now come. When the flag-of-truce boat landed within the rebel lines, the two systems confronted each other. On one side, hundreds of feeble, emaciated men, ragged, filthy, hungry, diseased, and dying; on the other an equal number of strong and hearty men, clad in the army clothing of the Government against which they had fought, having been humanely sheltered, fed, cleansed of dirt, cured of wounds and disease, and now honorably returned to fight that Government again.

The public sentiment of the North, outraged as it may have been, would never have permitted any other than this Christian and magnanimous course.

VII.

The three points now investigated — The conclusion of the Commissioners — These privations and sufferings were designedly inflicted — The late appeal to Divine and human judgment upon their cause by the rebel government — The spirit of that cause identical with the spirit which originated and defends it.

SUCH are the facts which have been brought to light by the inquiry of the Commissioners.

There were three points before them to be investigated. They were requested to ascertain "the true physical condition of the prisoners recently discharged by exchange from confinement at Richmond and elsewhere." They were also requested to ascertain whether these prisoners "did in fact, during such confinement, suffer materially for want of food, or from its defective quality, or from other privations and sources of disease."

This duty has been performed, and the result is now before the public.

There was one other point which the Commissioners were requested to make clear: "Whether the privations and sufferings of the prisoners were *designedly* inflicted on them by military or other authority of the rebel government, or were due to causes which such authorities could not control."

This question has already been alluded to digressively, but its full answer properly belongs to this stage of the narrative, when the whole field of the investigation is before the reader.

The feeling lingered in the minds of the Commissioners as the investigation went on, that this dreadful condition of things might be attributable to even other causes than the possible destitution of the rebel government. This latter consideration, it will be remembered, was, at an early moment, entirely disposed of. Any unconscious or unintentional form of crime is less reprehensible than that which is knowingly or deliberately committed. The question therefore suggested itself whether all this might not have been owing to the negligence and incompetence incident to an immature social system, or to the thoughtlessness of a reckless people, or to the mismanagement of an improvident government. This was the only alternative, and was sufficiently discreditable. But it was altogether more probable that a whole people and government could unite in being thoughtlessly and inconsiderately cruel, than consciously and purposely so. The latter was something too revolting to be entertained or believed. The whole current of public feeling and public principle generated by the spread of Christianity, and the progress of civilization, is so averse to anything of the kind that the majority of people are made almost incapable of comprehending, or even imagining such a state of mind in any community.

And yet it is to this very conclusion that every one must come who carefully weighs the testimony. Every doubt and misgiving successively disappears. No other theory will cover the immensity and variety of that system of abuse to which our soldiers are subjected. That abuse is, in all its forms, too general, too uniform, and too simultaneous to be otherwise than the result of a great arrangement. One prison-station is like another — one hospital resembles another hospital. This has been made especially apparent by intelligence that has reached the public just as this investigation is closing, and this report is being written. The remote prison at Tyler, in Texas, sends out a tale of suffering identical with that described in these pages. It was only a few weeks ago, that the streets of New Orleans beheld a regiment of half-starved and half-naked men, who had just been released from that station. Still more heart-rending is the later account, given in a memorial to the President, from Andersonville, Georgia, and in the full description, verified on oath, of what is now being suffered there by the imprisoned soldiers of our army. It would appear to be Belle-Isle five times enlarged, and ten-fold intensified. An enormous multitude of thirty-five thousand men are crowded together in a square enclosure or stockade of about twenty-five acres, with a noxious swamp at the centre, occupying one-fourth of the whole space. Here the prisoners suffer not only the privations already mentioned, but others peculiar to circumstances of a worse description.* In this pestilential prison they are dying at the rate of one hundred and thirty a day, *on an average!* The Commissioners allude to this station not as part of the evidence taken by themselves, but as an interesting, authentic, and corroborative illustration of the point now under consideration.

It is the same story everywhere; — prisoners of war treated worse than convicts, shut up either in suffocating buildings, or in outdoor enclosures, without even the shelter that is provided for the beasts of the field; unsupplied with sufficient food; supplied with food and water injurious and even poisonous; compelled to live in such personal uncleanliness as to generate vermin; compelled to sleep on floors often covered with human filth, or on ground saturated with it; compelled to breathe an air oppressed with an intolerable stench; hemmed in by a fatal dead-line, and in hourly danger of being shot by unrestrained and brutal guards; despondent even to madness, idiocy and suicide; sick of diseases (so congruous in character as to appear and spread like the plague) caused by the torrid sun, by decaying food, by filth, by vermin, by malaria, and by cold; removed at the last moment, and by hundreds at a time, to hospitals corrupt as a sepulchre, there, with few remedies, little care and no sympathy, to die in wretchedness and despair, not only among strangers, but among enemies too resentful either to have pity or to show mercy.

These are positive facts. Tens of thousands of helpless men have been and are now being disabled and destroyed by a process as certain as poison, and as cruel as the torture or burning at the stake, because nearly as agonizing and more prolonged. This spectacle is daily beheld and allowed by the rebel government.

No supposition of negligence, or thoughtlessness, or indifference, or accident, or inefficiency, or destitution, or necessity, can account for all this. So many and such positive forms of abuse and wrong cannot come from negative causes.

The conclusion is unavoidable, therefore, that "these privations and sufferings" have been "designedly inflicted by the military and other authority of the rebel government," and cannot have been "due to causes which such authorities could not control."

Further than this, the Commissioners are not required to express an opinion. Whether

* For the full account see Supplement, page 74.

or not they are the result of an infuriated and vindictive animosity against the Federal government and people, or the result of a pre-determined policy, deliberately formed, to discourage and affright our soldiers, to destroy them, or to disable them for further military service, or to compel our Government to an exchange on other than the terms to which it is in honor and by necessity committed, the public are in a position to decide.

The Commissioners have now performed their painful task. It has not been a grateful duty to narrate facts so unworthy of any people, especially of one heretofore so highly respected, so much admired, and in so many respects a credit to the American name. That name is shamed and dishonored by their exposure.

But there is one source of pride and congratulation; that, whatever abuses may have been developed on the Northern side of this war, none of them were originated or sanctioned by the government. In every case they have been the impulsive acts of subordinates here and there; and such are incident to any conflict. The noble and magnanimous manner in which the government treats the enemies to its peace and prosperity, when they have become helpless prisoners in its hands, is, alone, a sufficient manifestation of the spirit which animates it in waging this war. No sentiment of anger or resentment has actuated it from the beginning. The condition of its prison stations and hospitals is the best and proudest exponent of the cause of humanity which it seeks to maintain. This praise will be awarded it by the historian and by posterity, when the story of this stupendous struggle shall be written.

Can as much be said of the cause which stands in opposition to it? The facts of this narrative, and of others that will be yet more complete, will also enter into the future history of this conflict, but will form its most tragical chapter. It will in that day be known whether the spirit which animates the South is not also the spirit which has generated the cause of the South. The spirit which animates a cause gives the character to that cause. A people like an individual is estimated by its actions and by its motives.

Perhaps the world will yet discover a strange and reciprocal working of influences in the production of that which now opposes the republican progress of this government.

Perhaps the social theory, already so widely accepted, may yet be fully established, which attributes the alienation of the Southern people to a simple difference of feeling on a question of humanity. A too positive denial of humanity to another race, and a too positive contempt for a poorer class of their own race, have fostered those perverted principles, which would undermine a government filled with a more generous idea, and excite a hatred toward the people who would uphold it. As an exponent of the inhumanity of the Southern cause, it is not unjust, therefore, to point to its prisons and hospitals, where disregard of the sacredness of human life, and the cry of human suffering, has such an extraordinary manifestation.

And in the face of all this, the confederate congress, with the approval of the confederate president, issued, on the 14th of June last, a manifesto, of which the following is the concluding declaration:

"*We commit our cause to the enlightened judgment of the world, to the sober reflections of our adversaries themselves, and to the solemn and righteous arbitrament of Heaven.*"

Can this appeal, to both Divine and human judgment, be really sincere, or is it only a rounded and rhetorical termination of a state paper? Is the rebel government really so unconscious of this barbarous warfare, that it confidently expects the respect and sympathy of the civilized world? Is it really so unconscious of vindictive cruelty, that it confidently expects a revulsion in its favor from a community whose fathers and brothers and sons lie piled by thousands in pits and trenches, not on the battle-field but in the neighborhood of prisons and hospitals? Is it really so unconscious of crime that it claims even the favorable judgment of Him, unto whom all hearts are open, from whom no secrets are hid, and who requires of man to deal justly and to love mercy? Is it really anxious to stand before that bar whose final discrimination between good and evil it has been revealed, shall rest upon the single fact of humanity or inhumanity, whether the passions of anger and hate have been controlled, whether enemies have been forgiven, whether privation and suffering have been relieved? In view of the powerless captive, hungry, naked, sick and wounded, does it really await "the solemn and righteous arbitrament" of Him, to-day, who will hereafter say to the cruel and the unmerciful:

"I was an hungered, and ye gave Me no meat: I was thirsty, and ye gave Me no drink: I was a stranger, and ye took Me not in: naked and ye clothed Me not: sick and in prison, and ye visited Me not"?

Let the Southern conscience listen! Let it remember that the judgment of Heaven is on the side of humanity, and against cruelty and oppression; that a wrong done to a man is a wrong done to God, who will make the cause of the suffering His own, and will avenge Himself on His enemies:

"Verily, I say unto you, Inasmuch as ye

did it not to one of the least of these, ye did it not to Me!"

And here the Commissioners leave the subject. Their inquiry was originated, and has been pursued, in the hope that it might, by awakening further attention, be one of the means which would bring about an abandonment by the rebel government of its prison and hospital system. The many and simultaneous exposures which have been made, may possibly induce, at least, a prudence which may work the same result as a better motive. Already there are symptoms of some such movement, and of an admission, even at this late moment, of the misery that has been produced, a movement and admission whether made from necessity or self-interest does not yet appear.*

* It has not been thought necessary to allude to the subject of the suspension of the cartel of exchange, as it had but little bearing on the points to be investigated. But the lately published letter from Major General Butler, Commissioner of Exchange, to the Confederate Commissioner, Ould, is of interest and importance at the present juncture. It will be found printed entire in the supplement.
The following extract from General Butler's letter

But whatever the event may be, this inquiry will have worked its best purpose, if its facts should ever reach that nobler portion of the Southern people, who are really chivalrous and really religious, who have not been committed to these abuses, who have been kept in ignorance of them, and lead to a protest and revulsion that will compel their government to a repudiation of the iniquity, and to a course more worthy of a civilized and christian people.

has a connection with the above remark in the report:
"I unite with you cordially, Sir, in desiring a speedy settlement of all these questions, in view of the great suffering endured by our prisoners in the hands of your authorities, of which you so feelingly speak. Let me ask, in view of that suffering, why you have delayed eight months to answer a proposition, which, by now accepting, you admit to be right, just, and humane, allowing that suffering to continue so long? One cannot help thinking, even at the risk of being deemed uncharitable, that the benevolent sympathies of the Confederate authorities have been lately stirred by the depleted condition of their armies, and a desire to get into the field, to effect the present campaign, the hale, hearty, and well-fed prisoners held by the United States, in exchange for the half-starved, sick, emaciated, and unserviceable soldiers of the United States now languishing in your prisons."

The following paper having been read before the Commission, by Dr. WALLACE, it was, on motion of Dr. DELAFIELD, adopted by the Commission, and ordered to be appended to their Report.

MEDICAL REPORT.

Food — Quantity of Food for a Man — Character of Food — Relation of Food to Temperature — Ration of the Soldiers — Treatment of Rebel Prisoners at U. S. Stations — Rations — Clothing, Shelter and Fuel — Condition of Rebel Prisoners — Treatment of Union Prisoners in Rebel Hands — Rations of Union Prisoners — Quantity of Ration — Character and Quality of the Ration — Ill Effects of the Rations — No Variety in rations of Union Prisoners — Comparison of rations of Union and of Rebel Prisoners — Consequence of Deficient Food — Diseases Produced by Insufficient Food — Insufficient nutriment is Starvation — Privations other than of Food — Crowd Poisoning — Uncleanliness Compelled — Condition of Union Prisoners — Clothing and Warmth vs. Starvation — The Sick and Feeble liable to Freeze — Men Frozen — Numbers diseased as above — Management of the Sick — Starvation in Flanders — Cause of condition and Mortality of returned Union Prisoners — Treatment of Sick Union Prisoners — Mortality in Rebel Hospitals for Union Prisoners — Mortality in U. S. A. Hospital — Mortality at Belle Isle — Mortality at Andersonville — Mortality at Fort Delaware — Mortality at Johnson's Island — Additional Mortality — Kindness of Rebel Surgeons.

To Dr. VALENTINE MOTT, Chairman, etc.
MR. CHAIRMAN:—

According to the direction of the Commission, I lay before you certain considerations relating to the treatment adopted by the authorities of the States in rebellion towards United States soldiers held by them as prisoners of war, with the view of determining the influence of this treatment upon the hygiene and mortality of its subjects. I shall ground my remarks upon the evidence appended — upon the opinions of reliable scientific authorities — and to some, though slight degree, upon our own personal observation.

Food.

In investigating the subject before us, the question of *food* takes rank as of first importance; and, in considering this point, there are certain well established facts relating to the subject of alimentation, to which we must refer.

Quantity of Food for a man.

In deciding upon the quantity of food requisite for the due support of a man, Professor Dalton* says that "any estimate of the total quantity should state also the kind of food used," as the total quantity will necessarily vary with the quality, since some articles contain much more alimentary material than others." And Surgeon-General Hammond†

Character of Food.

says, "it is necessary that the food of man should consist of a *variety of substances*, in order that the several functions of the organism may be properly carried on; no fact in dietetics is better established than this." And Professor Dunglison‡ speaks to the same end thus: "man is so organized as to be adapted for living on both animal and vegetable substances, and if we lay aside our mixed nutriment, and restrict ourselves wholly to the products of the one or the other kingdom, scurvy supervenes.§

Dalton states that the amount of solid food required during twenty-four hours by a man in full health and taking free exercise in the open air, is, of bread, nineteen ounces; meat, sixteen ounces; and butter, three and a half ounces; in all, thirty-eight and a half ounces." Hammond places the amount of solid food "required to maintain the organism of a healthy adult American, up to the full measure of physical and mental capability, at about forty ounces, of which two-thirds should be vegetable, and one-third animal."

Moreover, due *variety in the food* is but second in importance to sufficient quantity. (See Pereira on food and diet.) In fact, the last named physiologist declares that "no matter how nutritious food may be, it is far better to exchange it for that even less nutritious, than to continue an unvarying sameness."

Relation of food to temperature.

And as to the relation of food to temperature: "In temperate climates, the *seasons* exercise an influence, not only over the quality, but the quantity of food taken into the system. Most persons eat more in winter than in summer. The cause is doubtless to be found in the fact, that, in cold weather a greater quantity of respiratory food is required in order to keep up the animal heat, than in hot weather, when the external temperature more nearly approaches the temperature of the body.‖ "He who is well fed," observes Sir John Ross, "resists cold better than the man who is stinted, while the starvation from cold follows but too soon a starvation in food." And Sir John Franklin, in his narrative of a journey to the Polar sea, writes, "no quantity of clothing could keep us warm while we fasted." "In tropical climates and in hot seasons, the system requires a smaller quantity of food than in colder countries and in cold seasons." * Individuals whose business requires much bodily exertion, or that they should spend much of their time in the open air, eat more than those of sedentary habits. And we have, from the authority of Carpenter, in his work on Human Physiology, that "a considerable reduction in the amount of food sufficient for men in regular active exercise, is, of course, admissible where little bodily exertion is required, and where there is less exposure to low temperatures."

Ration of the soldier.

The ration of the British Soldier is, at home stations, sixteen ounces of bread and twelve ounces of uncooked meat; at foreign stations, four ounces more of meat are allowed. Any extras are bought by the soldier out of his own funds. The French soldier in the Crimea had forty-two and five-eighths ounces of solid food, about ten and a half ounces of which were animal, the rest vegetable. In time of peace his ration is less. "The American soldier is better fed than any other in the world. This is proved by the healthy condition of the troops. Scurvy, one of *the first diseases to make its appearance when the food is of inferior quality*, has prevailed to so slight an extent, &c."† His ration of solid food‡ is about fifty-two and a half ounces, with a fair range for *variety*; and extra issues of pickles, fruits, and special vegetables, are made, when the medical officers deem them necessary. This ration is more than the man is generally able to consume, and the surplus is resold to the government for his benefit.

Treatment of Rebel Prisoners at U. S. Stations.—Rations.

The rations *issued* for the rebel soldiers held by our government as prisoners of war, were the same as for the United States garrison troops and soldiers on active service, except the bread ration, which was four ounces less; and the amount *given*, was, of solid food, forty-three ounces, besides extra vegetables, etc., sometimes, which were (see Captain Clark's evidence) procured by sale of the surplus, as above noted in the case of the Federal troops. No material change was made until the first of June, 1864, since which date the amount *given* was reduced to

---

* Human Physiology.
† Treatise on Hygiene.
‡ Human Health.
§ Professor Wood, in his Treatise on Practice of Medicine, defines *Scurvy* to be a disease in which "the blood is depraved, and the system debilitated, with a tendency to hemorrhage and to local congestions."
‖ Hammond's Hygiene.

* Pereira, Food and Diet.
† Hammond's Hygiene.
‡ Assuming soft bread and fresh beef as the basis.

thirty-four and a half ounces, while the range for variety of articles remained unchanged, and from the excess of the rations issued, the surplus fund for the use of the prisoners was larger than before. That this amount will be sufficient for comfort and health in the warm weather, and under the inactive life of the prisoner, we must infer from the statements of Pereira, Hammond, and Carpenter (above), and may likewise consider proven by the fact, that at Fort Delaware, even in the cold weather of the past winters, the prisoners could not consume all that was given them, and that large quantities of food were secreted, and wasted by them.* By authority of the War Department, the same REGULATIONS as are observed at all stations, where prisoners of war are held,† and of course at all such stations, the same general condition of things must prevail.

Clothing, shelter, and fuel.

Our evidence exhibits that all needful *clothing* and *blankets*, in some cases even to excess, as well as good and adequate *shelter*, with sufficient *fuel* for comfortable warmth, were furnished by the United States Government to the rebel prisoners.

Condition of Rebel Prisoners.

In our visit to Fort Delaware we passed through the barracks and enclosures containing about eight thousand prisoners. We observed that these men were in good physical condition, and presented the aspect of health and strength; as was the case at other stations, as seen by the appended evidence. The careful attention to cleanliness urged, and sometimes even enforced, by the United States officers in charge, doubtless contributes to their general good condition in no small degree. We were unable to observe any difference between the treatment of the rebels and the United States soldiers in the hospital at Fort Delaware, or in Lincoln Hospital near Washington. The evidence proves the same arrangements of ward, and bed, and diet, to have been made, with all other necessary appliances, for the rebel as for the Union soldier, in the time of sickness, at all stations where prisoners of war are held by the United States Government.

Treatment of Union Prisoners in rebel hands.

When we come to investigate the testimony in relation to the treatment of United States soldiers while prisoners in the hands of the rebels, we find a most serious difference from the state of things above described.

Rations of Union prisoners.

We learn from those returned that the rations given them varied at different times and places, but their declarations all concur in this, that they had not *food* enough to sustain their strength, nor to satisfy their hunger; and though these men were held captive at various times, and for a varying period, and at various places, yet their average statements are the same with little limitation.

Quantity of ration.

Wheat bread was given to some of them for a short time, but the bread was generally made of corn meal. The largest daily ration of wheat bread, of which we have evidence, would weigh about eleven (11) ounces, and the smallest but little more than three (3) ounces. The largest daily ration of corn bread was in bulk from thirty-one (31) to thirty-two (32) cubic inches, representing rather more than twelve (12) ounces of corn meal, while the smallest represented but four (4) ounces. The ration of meat was, in a few instances, from four (4) to six (6) ounces, but generally about two ounces, though in some cases it was less than this.

The meat was irregularly given; not often daily, and to some, only at intervals of days, or even several weeks, and when meat was served, the bread was, in many instances, diminished.

About half a pint of soup, containing sweet potato, or generally beans or peas in amount about two ounces, was sometimes given, with or without meat in different cases. The beans and peas were occasionally given raw and dry.

The maximum amount of solid food for one day, described, was . . 10 oz. bread.
                                      6 oz. beef.
With half a pint of soup made of the water in which the beef was boiled, and containing about two ounces of beans or peas, and, therefore representing . . . . . 2 oz.

Total, ... 18 oz.

The minimum amount was about . . . . . 4 oz. bread.
             . . . . . 1 oz. beef.

Total, ... 5 oz.

And so between five (5) and eighteen (18) ounces the rations varied, and in the article of meat, especially, was the great deficiency.

Character and Quality of the Ration.

But it is necessary to note the character also of the rations. The quality of the wheat bread appears to have been good, but that of the corn bread decidedly the reverse. It was made of meal which was

---
* See also letter from Quartermaster-General Meigs, appended.
† See Appendix.

coarsely ground and rough, contained all the hull (or bran), often whole grains of corn, with fragments of cob or of husk intermingled; frequently ill-baked, or over-baked, and sour and musty withal.

The soup was, by universal declaration of the witnesses, repulsive in odor and disgusting in flavor. It appears to have been made of the water in which the beef was boiled. Gravel and sand were the least objectionable of the impurites found in it.

The beans and peas issued were generally worm-eaten, and contained these insects in quantities, so that they would be floating on the surface, or intermixed throughout the mass of soup and beans.

Ill effects of the Rations.

Dunglison, in the work before quoted, says that "Corn bread, with those unaccustomed to its use, is apt to produce diarrhœa, in consequence *probably* of the presence of the husk,* with which it is always more or less mixed, &c.," and it is "but little adapted for those liable to bowel affections, &c. And Dr. Hassall says, "In those unaccustomed to its use, maize is considered to excite and to keep up a tendency to diarrhœa."

Every one is aware of the laxative influence of so-called bran bread,† which is due to the physical action of the hull of the grain upon the delicate lining membrane of the stomach and bowels, acting thereupon as an excitant or irritant, though tempered by the bland influence of the wheaten flour. Now what must be the result when the meal is of *corn*, and coarse, and intermixed with hull and grain entire, with husk and cob in fragments, among our Northern troops, who are, for the most part, "unaccustomed to the use of corn meal"? We see by the evidence, that some of the men observed the influence of this bread, in producing the diarrhœa with which so many were afflicted.

The character of the soup, as above described, would stamp it as entirely unfit for food, and upon men already suffering from diarrhœa, the evil influence of such a compound is but too plainly to be imagined. The evidence shows that some could not eat it, though hungry to starvation.

No variety in Rations of Union Prisoners.

The average amount of meat allowed was so small that it is not worthy of special consideration; and as to the *variety* and *change* of diet, upon which all physiologists lay so great stress,—it is not in the Record,—*there was none of it.*

* Prof. Dunglison informs me that by the word *husk,* he intends to imply that which is commonly denominated *bran.*
† See Pereira, Food and Diet.

Comparison of rations of Union and of Rebel prisoners.

How do these amounts and qualities compare with the maximum forty-three ounces, or the minimum thirty-four and a half ounces, of standard Government food, of excellent quality, and abundant room for variety, and extra issue of fresh vegetables according to necessity, which the United States Government allows its prisoners? The question may be answered by contrasting the exhausted, the attenuated, the melancholy, the imbecile, the dying, and the dead, Union soldiers, returning home from Richmond, with the cheerful, healthy, and vigorous Southerners, held at, or released from, the various United States stations referred to in the appended testimony.

Consequence of deficient food.

Let us look now at the consequence of deficiency of food, as explained by students and observers of the subject.

In the Medical and Surgical history of the British army which served in Turkey and the Crimea, we find that "during January, 1855, by the deficiency of food, the efficiency of the whole army was seriously compromised. Disease was simply the more overt manifestation of a pathological state of the system, which was all but universal, and merely indicated the worst grades of it. *Fever* and *affections of the bowels* represented the forms in which morbid actions were usually presented, while *gangrene* and *scurvy* indicated *those privations and that exposure* from which these diseases were mainly derived." Again, "in starvation the tissues of the body are consumed for the production of heat, and rapid loss of weight is the consequence. The other vital processes all involve decomposition of the substance of organs, and add to the loss which the body undergoes. From insufficient food *for a few*

Diseases produced by insufficient food.

weeks, disease is almost invariably induced; *typhus* and *typhoid fever, scurvy* and *anæmia* are the consequences."* Dr. Carpenter, in his Human Physiology, says, "the prisoners confined in Mill Bank Penitentiary, in 1823, who had previously received an allowance of from thirty-one to thirty-three ounces of dry nutriment daily, had this allowance suddenly reduced to twenty-one ounces,—animal food being almost entirely excluded from the diet scale. They were at the same time subjected to a low grade of temperature, and to considerable exertion; in the course of *a few weeks* the health of a large proportion of the inmates began to give way. The first symptoms were loss of color, and diminution of health and strength, subsequently *diar-*

* Hammond's Hygiene.

rhœa, dysentery, scurvy, and lastly *adynamic fevers*, or headache, vertigo, convulsions, maniacal delirium, apoplexy, &c. After death, ulcerations of the mucous lining of the alimentary canal were very commonly found; fifty-two per cent. were thus affected. That the reduction of the allowance of food was the main source of the epidemic, was proved, * * * &c."

Insufficient nutrition is starvation.

We appeal here to Chossat's Inquiries, resulting in the proof of this curious effect of *insufficient nutriment*, that it produces an incapability of digesting even the small amount consumed. "So that, in the end, the results are the same as those of *entire deprivation of food*, the total amount of loss being almost exactly identical, but its rate being less."

Privations other than of food.

But in addition to a starvation diet, our evidence furnishes proof of confinement to overcrowded rooms, without proper ventilation—of want of *clothing*—want of *shelter*—and denial of suitable means of warmth, whether by *blankets* or by *fuel*, and this even during the fall, winter, and spring just passed.

Crowd-Poisoning.

"*Overcrowding, imperfect ventilation*, and *want of cleanliness*, are three conditions usually associated, and may be designated by the single term *Crowd-Poisoning*."* The evidence exhibits that about twenty square feet was, in some instances, all the superficial space permitted to each man confined in prison. And, on Belle Isle, it would appear that for a time there was little variation from the same area. "The air of crowded camps and habitations becomes contaminated through emanations given off during respiration, through effluvia from the skin, and by the decomposition of the various excreta. The nitrogenized matter carried into the air from the skin, and the products arising from the decomposition of the excreta, are sources of deadly mischief. The effects of overcrowding are not only manifested by the increased violence and the adynamic character of all diseases occurring among those exposed, but the development and severity of the adynamic fevers appear particuarly connected with this cause."† And again, "To the organic matters emanating from the human body, more than to any other cause, the injurious results of overcrowding are to be ascribed."

"The proofs are ample, that the emanations from the human body are of a decidedly deleterious character, when present in large amounts in the atmosphere inhaled. They are absorbed by the clothing, and even the walls of the room take them up and retain them for a long time." * "If animals be kept crowded together in ill-ventilated apartments, they speedily sicken." † "The continued respiration of an atmosphere charged with the exhalations of the lungs and skin is the most potent of all the predisposing causes of disease." ‡

Uncleanliness compelled.

But Dr. Woodward alludes to "want of cleanliness" as one of the elements of ordinary crowd-poisoning. Far more than ordinary was this "want" in the rebel prisons, especially on Belle Isle. A reference to the evidence will show that accumulation of filth of the most noisome character was compelled by prison discipline; that important accommodations were denied during the night hours, resulting in unavoidable soiling of the quarters of the prisoners, while the means of bathing, though convenient, were to so great an extent denied the prisoners, as to produce, in a large number of them, a condition of the skin, which is not only a disease in itself, but is also a cause of disorders various and grave. §

Condition of Union Prisoners.

We observed the surface of the bodies of a number who suffered thus; it was of most remarkable aspect, appearing as though it had been covered with a heavy coat of common varnish, which had dried, and cracked, and was pealing up in scales of every size. To the touch, it was as sand-paper of irregular quality. The cuticle—both effete and living—lay in masses, separated by fissures of varying extent and depth, through which watery and bloody fluids were seen exuding. The soles of the feet were like the sole of a plasterer's shoe—white, brown and yellow; the cuticle dried and broken, and laminated variously.

The functions of the skin, upon which physiologists lay so great stress, are here almost entirely unperformed, and hence we have "gastric disturbances, and diarrhœas," with suppression of that aeration of blood—that true respiration, which, physiologists tell us, takes place through the skin. Hence the lungs are overtaxed, and congestions are induced. And when to this we add the depraved state of the blood of the sufferers, and their exposures to cold, and wet, and storm, by day and night, we have, in full quantity, those general and special condi-

---

* Woodward; Camp Diseases.
† Woodward.

* Hammond.
† Dunglison.
‡ Carpenter.
§ See Surgeon Ely's evidence.

tions, which induce pulmonary diseases of every grade and character.

Clothing and warmth vs. starvation.

On the question of clothing and warmth; from what has been shown above, a corollary is directly deducible, viz.: That if food be in limited quantity, low temperature should be avoided, and external warmth duly maintained. "Artificial warmth may be made to take the place of nourishment otherwise required. And there is adequate ground for considering death by *starvation*, as really death from *cold*. The temperature of the body is maintained with little diminution till the fat is consumed, and then rapidly falls, unless it be kept up by heat externally applied."* Now not only was external heat not granted by the rebels to their prisoners, but their blankets were generally taken from them, as also some of their personal clothing.

The sick and feeble liable to freezing.

Further, "*the sick and feeble will not bear the low temperature, which, to those in good condition, acts as a healthful stimulant. In diseases attended with deficient power of circulation, congelation of the tissues* is liable to occur, from the effects of a temperature which could not give rise to it in a healthy subject." We see that diarrhœa, scurvy,— and these two disorders existing coincidently "in the majority of cases of diarrhœa,"— congestion of the lungs of atonic character, and "debilitas," (as the medical records of the hospital have it,) all stand out prominently in the evidence, as being an almost constant condition among those who have been prisoners in Danville, Va., Richmond, Va., and *especially on Belle Isle*. The authorities hereinbefore quoted show that these formidable disorders are the legitimate offspring of the treatment to which our men have been subjected while in the hands of the rebels. Shall we be surprised that diseases obey the laws of their production, or that they flourish, luxuriant and rank, in a soil specially prepared for their reception? And are not all these "diseases attended with deficient power of circulation"? Are not the subjects of the same "sick and feeble"? Is it all surprising that they cannot bear the low temperature of a winter on Belle Isle,—clad only in worn-out or scanty clothing,—with inadequate or with no shelter,— with little fire, or generally none at all,—and having no resting place but the ground, in mud and frost and snow? Nay, is it not a cause for wonder that "congelation of the tissues" was not even more common among them? Our evidence tells of many men freezing on Belle Isle, to loss of limb, and more, of life.

* Carpenter.

Men frozen.

We saw cases of "amputation by frost," at the United States Hospitals, at Baltimore, and Annapolis, and the "Quarterly Report of the hospitals for the Federal prisoners, Richmond, Va.," (appended,) shows that of two thousand seven hundred and seventy-nine patients admitted in January, February, and March, 1864, there were fifteen cases of gelatio, (or freezing,) and fifty of gangrene from frozen feet! And from the same

Numbers diseased as above.

document we find that two thousand one hundred and twenty-one, out of the two thousand seven hundred and seventy-nine, were affected with debility, adynamic fevers, diarrhœa, dysentery, diseases of the chest, and scurvy—the very effects proved above to be produced by starvation, cold, overcrowding, filth, and exposure; and, as already mentioned, the testimony of the United States surgeons at Annapolis and Baltimore shows that the great majority of our soldiers received from rebel prisons suffered under the same affections. These surgeons further

Management of the sick.

declare, that these diseases did not yield to ordinary medical treatment; that they were most successfully managed by "*nullifying the cause*," that is, by nutrition and stimulation, with especial attention to cleanliness and fresh air, medical agencies being only accessories, and sometimes not resorted to at all.

Starvation in Flanders.

M. Fleury (cours d'hygiene) says: "Sous le nom de *fièvre de famine*, M. de Meersman a tracé un tableau complet et méthodique de *l'état morbide que développe l'alimentation insuffisante*, et qu'il dit avoir observé en 1846 et 1847 dans les Flandres belges." He then recounts the article, which is too long to bear quotation here, but it is a most singularly accurate description of that which our soldiers returned from rebel prisons state in regard to their own feelings and sufferings,—of those conditions which the United States surgeons at the Baltimore and Annapolis hospitals have delineated to us,—and which we witnessed and observed in our visits to the institutions above mentioned.

Cause of condition and mortality of returned Union prisoners.

It is utterly incorrect to charge the bodily attenuation, the mental imbecility, and the startling mortality which prevail so largely among the men from the prisons of the South, upon the mere diseases of which they are the subjects. If a man swallow a poisonous dose of arsenic, he will suffer pain, vomiting, diarrhœa, hæmorrhages, and convulsions, even unto death; are these "more overt manifestations,"—these necessary consequen-

ers of the morbific agent applied,—to be considered as the causes of the death? Or shall we go to the true first cause direct, and say "the man died by poisoning by arsenic"?

So have our men died,—from cold and exposure, from crowd poisoning, from starvation and from privation, while the way to death was roughly paved with disease of body and of mind,—mere minor manifestations of those allied powers of evil.

Treatment of sick Union prisoners.

But we further find a similar treatment,—similar in kind, though modified in degree,—dealt out to the wounded and the sick on Belle Isle and in Richmond. The evidence of those who have been under the care of the surgeons at these stations is corroborated by the testimony of Colonel Farnsworth, and by that of Surgeons Ferguson and Richards. The latter lay stress upon the offensive, and "utterly unfit," character of the beds and bedding, and declare that the diet was "entirely insufficient to give them a proper chance of recovery," and state further that there was a deficiency of medical supplies in the hospital for Federal prisoners, while the evidence is before us that at General Hospital No. 4, Richmond, the *Confederate soldier* had "as much good food as he could eat, with good bedding and sheets;" and evidence to the same end appears in relation to "Confederate hospitals in the field."

Mortality in Rebel Hospitals for Union Prisoners.

On the subject of the mortality of Union prisoners in rebel hands, we find that the "Quarterly Report," above referred to, exhibits a record, which, though startling and fearful, is yet easily explained by the foregoing considerations. For what can be expected of men worn out, almost unto death, by the want of those things which are necessary for the body,—and then further reduced by disease,—when subjected to such privations and noxious influences as those described by Surgeons Ferguson and Richards? This "Report" shows a mortality among the sick of rather more than fifty per cent!* How does this compare with that at the United States General Hospital at Annapolis which is only eighteen per cent?

Mortality in U. S. A. Hospital.

Yet the cases at Annapolis were all brought by flag-of-truce boat from City Point, Virginia, and were of the same general class as those in the "Hospitals for the Federal Prisoners, Richmond, Virginia."

Mortality at Belle Isle.

Further, we find that "a Confederate official, whose evidence cannot be questioned, declared that of the numbers remaining at Belle Isle, then about eight thousand (8,000), about twenty-five died daily, and that it would be but a few weeks before the deaths would count fifty a day." From this, we have a mortality at Belle Island in a ratio of *one hundred and fourteen per cent. per year*, with double this amount in prospect.

Mortality at Andersonville.

Again; the *Macon Journal and Messenger* says that "there are now over twenty-seven thousand (27,000) prisoners at Andersonville, Georgia, among whom the deaths are from fifty to sixty a day," or in a ratio of about from *sixty-eight to eighty-one per cent. per year.*

Mortality at Fort Delaware.

Turn now to the mortality among the rebel prisoners at Fort Delaware, where, in addition to the more ordinary causes of sickness and death among soldier-prisoners, we find "small-pox, the majority of the prisoners not having been vaccinated before they came here." Also, a "prostrated condition of the prisoners from Vicksburg, a great many of whom had to be carried, on their arrival here, from the boat to the hospital, and many of whom represented that they had been limited to half and quarter rations during the siege of Vicksburg;" and "prisoners from Vicksburg and the Mississippi Valley laboring under miasmatic influences, under which a great number of them died." Yet with all these extra causes of death, the mortality for the entire year just closed, amounts to less than *twenty-nine per cent.*, and when these special causes ceased to exist, it diminished rapidly, and during the three months of April, May, and June, it had fallen to *below a ratio of ten and a half per cent. per year*, and was still diminishing, while the sum total of prisoners was yet increasing.

Mortality at Johnson's Island.

Again; at Johnson's Island, Sandusky bay, Ohio,—the climate of which station has been stigmatized by our enemies as insalubrious, and in high degree pernicious to the constitution of the Southerner,—the deaths among the rebel prisoners during the year 1863, with the prevalence of measles and small-pox, amounted to *less than nine per cent.;* and during May and June of this year, there were but six deaths, that is, in the *ratio of less than two per cent. per year.*

By such contrasts of mortality at United States stations, and at rebel stations, argument and comment are struck dumb.

---

* Four deaths only occurred from wounds.

* Since this was written a sworn statement has come to our hands, (a copy of which will be found in the Supplement,) whence it appears that the mortality at Andersonville had increased rapidly, and had advanced in fact to a ratio from *one hundred and thirty-five to one hundred and fifty-two per cent. per year.*

Additional Mortality.

There are still others, who are destined to fall victims to what we are compelled by the evidence to consider a carefully devised plan for the destruction of Union soldiers, by weapons as surely, though not so mercifully, fatal, as shot and shell and bayonet. We refer to such, as, being broken down in mind and intellect, and vitiated in bodily vigor, and diseased beyond hope of recovery, by all the morbific causes which the rebel authorities have arrayed against them during their imprisonment,—and who being discharged from their country's service for disability,—will, in weeks and months to come, swell the local lists of mortality in the districts of their own homes.

Kindness of Rebel Surgeons.

We have been much gratified to find, not only from the sworn testimony, but from private conversation with a very large number of our returned prisoners, that the treatment and attention they received at the hands of the rebel surgeons was kind and sympathizing; their necessities were evidently as faithfully ministered to by these medical officers, (with one exception only), as the provision made by the authorities of the rebel government would allow.

Respectfully submitted,

ELLERSLIE WALLACE.

July, 1864.

TO THE READERS OF THE LIVING AGE,

AFTER THEY SHALL HAVE PERUSED THE REPORT OF THE SANITARY COMMITTEE

Now that you have read — with a sorrow and indignation which words cannot speak, and which can only be expressed by tears, and sobs, and teeth closely set together — the record of cruelties inflicted upon your fathers, and brothers, and sons who went forth at the call of their country to uphold her Constitution and Laws, — it is important that you should have a clear knowledge of the origin of these horrors.

They seem to have been prompted by fiendish malignity and ingenuity. But the perpetrators did not arise from the bottomless pit. They were born of women. They were originally like yourselves. And if subjected to the same temptations, you would become even as they are, and as many Northern men have already become.

These human beings (for such they are) have had their worst propensities magnified and inflamed by the possession of despotic and irresponsible power. Cut off, by their own intolerance and fierceness, from the society of all who believe in the Declaration of Independence, and from the influence of the public opinion of Christendom (of which they heard only enough to irritate them), they have herded together, and have "bred in and in" their defiance of the laws of God and man, and their hatred and cruelty, until they seem to have been delivered over to believe that they have a Divine right to do as they please, not only to their slaves, but to all mankind who differ from them.

These effects have legitimately flowed from Slavery. You must remove the cause, if you wish to have peace and union.

But this cause removed, by the blessing of Almighty God upon our armies, we shall dwell together in safety. The Capital and Industry of the Free States will make the South the Garden of America; will make her production an hundred-fold; and once more,

"As a band of brothers joined,
Peace and safety we shall find."

APPENDIX

TO THE

REPORT OF THE SANITARY COMMITTEE:

BEING THE

EVIDENCE TAKEN BY THE COMMISSION

RELATING TO

TREATMENT OF UNION PRISONERS BY THE REBELS.

EVIDENCE OF OFFICERS AND SOLDIERS OF THE UNITED STATES ARMY* RETURNED AFTER CONFINEMENT IN REBEL PRISONS.

Testimony taken at Annapolis, Maryland, at United States Army General Hospital, Division No. 1, May 31, A.D. 1864.

COMMISSIONERS PRESENT.—Dr. Valentine Mott, Dr. Edward Delafield, Gouverneur M. Wilkins, Esq., Dr. Ellerslie Wallace, Hon. J. I. Clarke Hare, Rev. Treadwell Walden.

TESTIMONY OF PRIVATES AND NON-COMMISSIONED OFFICERS.

Private JOSEPH GRIDER, *sworn and examined:*—

I come from East Tennessee, near Knoxville; enlisted in the 3d East Tennessee infantry. I was taken prisoner near home, betrayed by a citizen, 30th October, 1863. I was taken to Atlanta, Georgia, and then taken to Richmond. I am fifty-eight years of age; my health was pretty good when I was last captured. The first time I was balled and chained at Macon, Georgia. I escaped from Macon, Georgia; was taken as a spy; some papers found on me — recruiting papers. Was put in Libby Prison first, kept there about three weeks, then was removed to Danville. I first escaped August 31st, and afterwards was retaken. I then had my uniform on as I had before when I was taken as a spy. When I reached Richmond my health was only tolerable good, which was occasioned by the treatment I had previously received. During while I was escaping I lived on stolen corn and stolen pigs; I broiled the meat in the mountains; I was in Libby about three weeks; was in Danville over five months. Left Danville 16th of April to come here.

In Libby my daily ration was corn bread — very rough. It was not sieved — plenty of whole grains in it; (witness gives the measure, which amounts to about 31† cubic inches). There were corn husks also in the bread as large as my two fingers. I kept a journal, but it was taken from me; it was in the haversack. Had meat sometimes, about every other day, about two ounces. The bread weighed from a half pound to three-quarters — for two men — as some of our men weighed it. I could have eat up my rations and my partner's and not had enough at that, when I was well. It was just the diet that made me sick; the bread was not done half the time.

Everything was taken from me but my dress coat, shirt, pants and boots; slept on the floor; walked many a night to keep warm; there were two hundred and fourteen men in the room I staid in; we laid close together, about a foot apart.

Rations at Libby not the same as at Danville; at Danville we got black bread, which we drew until it gave out, then we had corn bread. There were lots of men who walked

---

* The term "United States Army" is used here and elsewhere for convenience, and includes both the regular and volunteer service.

† Representing a fraction more than twelve ounces of raw corn meal.

all night to keep warm. At Danville we got bigger of the black bread than common; I threw it up, I couldn't eat it. It is made of cane seed; I never knew it to be eaten before. I was in Danville about four weeks before the diarrhœa came on me; I had lost flesh before and since my capture. My healthy weight is from two hundred and twelve to two hundred and fourteen pounds.

I went into the hospital when I had the diarrhœa; there got pea-soup and a slice of white bread, size of half my hand. I found bugs in the soup, that was boiled out of the peas. I was there twelve days before they gave me any medicine, or told me what was the matter with me.

My diarrhœa had stopped some time before I was exchanged; I afterwards had the pleurisy. I have gained flesh since I came here. They abuse the Tennesseans worse than other prisoners. Our food was about the same.

They would not let you look out the windows. They shot seven men for looking out; one was shot on my floor; his name was Robert McGill; he got well; he had just put his hand out to throw out some water.

It was warm enough in the day-time when we were stirring about. Sometimes we were allowed to go to the privy and sometimes we were not. We have been kept from it so much as three days, until we fouled the floor — this was for punishment for taking a little slat or such thing, by those who were on the lower floor. I can eat two such corn cakes as I got.

JOSEPH GRIDER.

Sworn to and subscribed before me,
May 31st, 1864.
D. P. BROWN, JR.,
United States Commissioner.

Private JACKSON O. BROSHERS, *sworn and examined:*—

Age, twenty years; height, six feet one inch; ordinary weight from one hundred and seventy to one hundred and seventy-five pounds. I have weighed but one hundred and sixty pounds; improved for a while in weight in the army. I enlisted from Spencer county, Indiana, in the 65th Indiana; captured December 16th; in prison at Belle Isle, and at Pemberton buildings in Richmond.

Was clad with great coat and blanket when taken. They were taken from me; they gave me no blankets or covering. I wore a jacket, shirt, drawers, &c., while in prison. The prison was not a very good place to stay; it was a tent; I staid in it at Belle Isle; the rain came in; suffered from the cold; it was cold weather; had some little fire part of the time; I had a Sibley tent very much torn; the fire was in the centre.

I saw a good many men — over three hundred — without shelter for some weeks; I slept on an old coat I got from a rebel; no man ever said he was comfortable in prison; our men would sleep upon what they could get; I have a chronic diarrhœa; had corn bread in prison; before I came away they gave us more; I had enough for a while of such as was given us; no whole grains in my bread; it was white corn bread; had pork once; don't know how often I had beef; don't think seven times; was in Belle Isle about two and a half months; got a piece of meat about the size of my two fingers. I judge it had worms in it by the holes I saw; before I came away, I got enough of such as it was, but at first I did not.

I lost my strength I think for the want of food; it was a month and a half that we had no meat; had not been sick before I entered the army; most of the men complained of being hungry; they appeared ravenous when the rations were brought in.

I have gained strength since I have been here; I have the diarrhœa; had it about two weeks before I came from prison; I think I lost my strength before the diarrhœa began; lost my flesh afterward; the worst of my weakness was after the diarrhœa commenced; could not have walked three miles without resting before the diarrhœa came on.

I did not suffer from the want of air, but the want of room; I suffered from cold a great deal; about fourteen to fifteen men sleep in a Sibley tent in our army.

I got some crackers that they said came from the Sanitary Commission, a cap, overcoat and canteen; the other men got some clothing, too, that they said came from the Sanitary Commission.

My rations were somewhat less than this bible.*

JACKSON O. BROSHERS.

Sworn to and subscribed before me,
May 31st, 1864.
D. P. BROWN, JR.,
United States Commissioner.

Corporal WILLIAM M. SMITH, *sworn and examined:*—

I am twenty-two years old; from Kentucky; enlisted in the 8th Kentucky regiment September 24th, 1861; was captured September 20th, 1863; taken to Richmond, Virginia; was captured at the battle of Chattanooga.

I was put in Smith's building, after being

---

* Which being measured, contains 31¼ cubic inches.

some six days at Belle Isle; in Smith's building about two months.

Had on good clothes when taken in; they took blankets and oil cloth, extra shirt and drawers, &c., from me; while we were in Richmond, there were some Sanitary clothes sent there; they were needed mighty bad; the rebels have taken a heap of Sanitary clothing, I think.

At Belle Isle, laid out on the naked ground; it rained some two days.

I took the small-pox in Danville; I was then taken to the hospital; I wore the same clothing I had before I got it; I wore the same clothes when I came on here; I believe I had a shirt and my dress coat washed; I washed my drawers myself.

I came here the second of May.

My health was pretty good when taken prisoner; when I left I was taken out of the hospital; I guess it was the small-pox, erysipelas and diarrhœa which brought me down.

When I was in prison, before I was taken sick, got a piece of corn bread about the size of this bible, (the same referred to by the other witness;) got meat three or four days in the week; when sick, got a small piece of wheat bread — as much as I could eat then — a piece of beef with it, about two ounces; sometimes a little beef soup, with red peas in it, and rice; we had coffee made out of rye — sometimes, once a day — most every day; I took the small-pox first; I was there about a week before I took it; felt pretty well before; did not get enough to eat before; hungry all the time.

WILLIAM M. SMITH.

Sworn to and subscribed before me,
May 31st, 1864.

D. P. BROWN, JR.,
United States Commissioner.

Sergeant ALFRED P. JONES, *sworn and examined:*—

I am twenty-seven years of age; am from Worcester, Massachusetts; I enlisted September 14th, 1861, in Boston, in the 1st Massachusetts cavalry; was taken prisoner in Virginia, at Aldie, June 17th, 1863; was taken to Libby prison June 24th, 1863.

Was in prison two days and one night; then taken to Belle Isle, and remained there some thirty days when I was exchanged; I was protected from the weather by a tent — it was full of holes; some were as well off and others were not — some laid on the bare ground — some four hundred; had no blanket or overcoat when I went there.

I sold my India rubber cover to a rebel to buy bread with.

A good many who went to the prison when I did, had their blankets taken from them; the men said they wanted the clothes for their own soldiers; I used to see the rebel officers dressed in our uniforms.

Most of the men seemed to have coughs, and were very weak.

The prisoners complained of a want of food; it was a general complaint; I walked the streets many a night; I could not sleep from hunger; all complained.

At the time I was there in June and July, 1863, the food was very fair, but in small quantities; received one-fourth of a loaf in the morning of wheat bread, which was three inches by three and three-fourths, by one and three-fourths. We had this twice a day; about two small mouthfuls of meat. For supper we had a half pint of bean soup; don't remember finding any worms in it; there would be sand or gravel in it; there was no deficiency in water. We were allowed to go out in squads to bathe. There were squads let out to bathe and wash their clothes.

I had nothing to sleep on; it was warm in the day time, cool at night.

I heard many complain of cramp and pains. I lost flesh and strength, and so did the others, from want of food.

ALFRED P. JONES,
Sergeant Co. C., 1st Massachusetts Cavalry.

Sworn to and subscribed before me,
May 31st, 1864.

D. P. BROWN, JR.
United States Commissioner.

Private WILLIAM D. FOOTE, *sworn and examined:*—

I was born in Canada, and enlisted in Buffalo, New York, on 31st October, 1862, in the 9th New York Cavalry; I am twenty-eight years of age; have been in the army about a year and eight months.

Was in the hands of the rebels about nine months; was at Belle Isle, and in the hospital at Richmond; was well when I was captured; I was taken with diarrhœa.

For first two or three months at Belle Isle the quality of rations was very good; hardly sufficient to sustain life in quantity. It was wheat bread, almost four inches square, not exceeding half an inch in thickness, a small portion of beef — call it two mouthfuls. We had this quantity of bread twice a day, and a small tincupful of bean soup, which had black bugs in it, which would float on the top. We then got corn bread, about half the size of this Bible, (the same one previously referred to,) twice a day.

I was seven weeks I had no shelter at all; the latter part of the time had a tent full of holes.

The latter part of October received blankets, &c., from our Government; my blankets and clothes had been taken from me.

I lost flesh. Out of seven hundred that came to Belle Isle with me, I think there were about two hundred got shelter; we were exposed to the weather.

There was no name for our hunger. When a bone would be thrown away by some, it would be taken up often by others, and boiled to get something out of it.

All who were there failed in strength and flesh as I did, from starvation, I think.

There were no sheds put up for us.

I should judge it was the corn bread which caused the diarrhœa. It appeared to disagree with me, for when I had wheat bread, I kept my health perfect. The corn bread gave me pain in my bowels; often got whole grains and husks in the bread, I am positive, as I am on my oath; the proportion would be small; after that, we got rye and corn mixed, of a better quality of bread.

WILLIAM D. FOOTE.

Sworn to and subscribed before me,
May 31st, 1864.
D. P. BROWN, JR.,
United States Commissioner.

Private ROBERT MORRISON, sworn and examined:—

I was enlisted from the northwest part of Ohio, in Pendleton, Putnam county, Riley township, in the 21st Ohio Volunteers; I was taken prisoner at Chattanooga, September 20th, 1863; I was removed to Richmond; was two or three days on our way; I was stout and healthy when I reached Richmond; I forget the name of the prison into which I was put — I remember, it was Pemberton; I remained there about a month, was then removed to Danville, Virginia, remained there till I was brought here; was placed in buildings at Danville.

Our blankets were taken from us; our other clothing was left to us: had no overcoat; had no watch; we saved our money; I put it in the sole of my boot; they searched us for it; we had a stove — got wood once in a while; it was not very comfortable.

My health was first-rate before I entered the service; I was in the army about nineteen months before I was captured; had no bowel complaint or any other sickness while in our army; when I went into the army my weight was one hundred and twenty-five pounds.

I got a chunk of corn bread daily, the size of this Bible*; it satisfied me and more too, because I couldn't eat it; sometimes it was but about half baked; it was of a yellow color; it was of a musty taste; had a very small ration of meat about as large as three of my fingers in breadth, and about two inches in thickness.

* The same before referred to.

I was about two months in prison before I took sick; my first sickness was fever and ague; I had not had it before for some years; I have a little bowel complaint now, it does not trouble me much; I had the lung fever afterwards. I got some eggs then; when I got so as to be up and around I was sent back to the prison; I then took the diarrhœa; that came on in about three weeks after my return to the prison; it reduced me down — was sent back to the hospital; got wheat bread then, an egg, small piece of meat, potatoes, salt meat, some soup not very good; there was rice in the soup; was in a bed when I had the lung fever; I could go into corn bread pretty fast at first; the meat was pretty good — fresh meat; I was there about six months; if the corn bread had been good, with the meat, it would have been plenty; had not been in the habit of eating corn bread; it was kind of musty. In the corn bread there were some grains of corn.

A hundred and fifty men in the room where I was. In a warm evening the room was very close; we had brooms to sweep the room; the privy was handy; the room we were in was about sixty by sixty feet; we had as much food as we wanted, such as it was.

There was about a foot between each man as we lay; we had a small yard we could walk around, about fifteen or sixteen feet wide, by one hundred and fifty feet long; I think it was the corn bread and fresh meat that gave me the bowel complaint; I was not used to the corn bread.

I am twenty-three years of age.
ROBERT MORRISON.

Sworn to and subscribed before me,
May 31, 1864.
D. P. BROWN, JR.,
United States Commissioner.

Testimony taken at United States Army General Hospital, Division No. 2, Annapolis, Maryland, May 31, 1864.

ALL THE COMMISSIONERS PRESENT.

Private GEORGE DINGMAN, sworn and examined:—

I am fifty-four years of age: I am from Michigan; enlisted in the 27th Regiment in 1862; I had always good health till captured; was taken at Strawberry Plain; taken to Richmond, thence to Belle Island about the 26th of January; had no shelter but the heavens; was taken by some one into a tent; had the rheumatism.

No shelter was provided by the authorities; some hundreds had no shelter, some had; no fire; had nothing to sleep on but them blankets I brought; had blankets when taken prisoner.

(A ration produced); this was the rations I got; sometimes we got this twice and sometimes three times a day (the ration weighs two ounces of bread and three-sixteenths of an ounce of meat; both are now perfectly dry which causes a loss of weight); have had meat more than once a day.

Was at Belle Isle two weeks; think the prisoners got a little more bread on the island than at the hospital; my ration was two inches in length by two and a half inches wide, and about one inch thick, three times a day, or twice a day sometimes; suffered from hunger; could not lay in bed from rheumatism; when the hungry feeling came I got so weak I could not walk; once and a while had a little soup or beans raw; no man could eat the soup unless he was starving; it tasted nasty and briny; I could walk when I came here, but had no strength.

I saw the rations the rebel guards got; they were four times as much as ours: they got the same kind of bread and meat, but they could help themselves out of the bag.

There were complaints; the doctor was very kind, and did all he could.

During January the men would run all night to keep warm, and in the morning I would see men lying dead; from three to six or seven; they were frozen; this was nearly every morning I was there; the men would run to keep warm, and then lie down and freeze to death; we made an estimate and found that seventeen men died a night from starvation and cold, on an average.

If I were to sit here a week I couldn't tell you half our suffering.

GEORGE DINGMAN.

Sworn to and subscribed before me,
May 31st, 1864.
D. P. BROWN, JR.,
United States Commissioner.

Private CHARLES H. ALLEN, sworn and examined: —

My home is in New York; enlisted in the 16th New York Regiment last fourth of July; was sickly then; don't know when I was captured; it was in Virginia; was taken to Belle Isle.

They took my clothes away; my extra clothing, my overcoat and blanket; it was at the end of the winter; slept on the ground; remained about two months without shelter, then went to the hospital.

It was cold; suffered a great deal with cold; some froze to death; I only saw dead men once.

We got corn bread and sometimes soup; corn bread twice a day; meat three or four times a week; I got a quarter of a loaf of corn bread for each ration about as wide as my four fingers, and about four fingers thick.

I was hungry, pretty nearly starved to death all the time.

Rations not as good at the hospital; not so large.

Had a frozen foot and diarrhœa when I went to the hospital; think it was the beans and water which gave me the diarrhœa; I relished the bread at first, then I lost my relish for it; was in Belle Isle about three months; from the last of the winter.

Was in Belle Isle two months before I froze my feet; I heard that a good many more were frozen to death; about sixty I suppose; I did not go round the tents, and therefore did not see them; I have lost the end of my little toe (witness exhibits his frozen toe to the Commission).

CHAS. H. ½ ALLEN.
his
mark.

Sworn to and subscribed before me,
May 31st, 1864.
D. P. BROWN, JR.,
United States Commissioner.

Private FRANK EICHELBERGER, sworn and examined: —

I am from Baltimore; enlisted August, 1861, in the 8th Kansas, Company A; captured at Chattanooga; health good up to that time; taken to Richmond and placed in a tobacco warehouse; I am twenty-two years of age; got to Richmond 21st of October; went into prison in December, and remained till March.

They took our blankets and coats away from us; laid on planks; on the floor; it was warm when we were crowded.

Got corn bread, rice, sweet potatoes; meat once a week; got rice and sweet potatoes every other day; corn bread three inches square, one and a half inches thick, twice a day; teacupful of rice; sometimes soup, two-thirds of a pint; we got soup about as often as we got meat.

It did not satisfy hunger; my appetite was never satisfied; my health declined rapidly.

I got a heavy cold; and then went to the hospital, when I had the pneumonia; the condition of the other men was about the same with regard to their food and accommodations; they complained of their treatment while at the hospital; got dried apples and coffee sent to us from the North.

I had no pain when I suffered from hunger; could not sleep on account of hunger; did not suffer from cold a great deal; the loaf shown to me is just like what we got; about one-third of it (loaf weighs fifteen ounces, and measured about thirty-one and a half cubic inches), twice a day.

The rebel guards got the same kind of bread; a great deal more; enough to satisfy any man's hunger; sometimes their bread was better than this; the bread was made of corn meal not sifted; no grains or cob in it that I saw; I believe some of our men did complain; haven't heard any reason why we were not better fed.

FRANK EICHELBERGER.

Sworn to and subscribed before me,
May 31st, 1864.
D. P. BROWN, JR.,
United States Commissioner.

Private DANIEL McMANN, *sworn and examined:* —

I am from New York; enlisted in the 43d New York; captured at Gettysburg; was sickly when captured; taken to Richmond; placed in Belle Isle.

Took my coat and blanket away; gave us no covering; some laid out on a bank; reached Belle Isle in July; a number of men had to lie out on the bare ground — two hundred; I was there till after Christmas.

I suffered from cold very much, and so did the men more than I; we had cold rain storms; some men froze to death in a ditch.

It was not much better in the tents; I saw men carried out of the tents in blankets, dead; saw this more than once; I suppose they died mostly from hunger and cold.

We got about one-third the loaf shown, of corn bread (loaf weighed, and weighs fifteen ounces) twice a day; sometimes but once; meat once regularly; a small piece about as big as my four fingers together.

Went into the hospital after Christmas, and remained till last of March; rations worse in hospital; as much bread, meat and soup given to us the same day at the hospital; they were bad and we could not eat them; a hungry man could not eat the meat and soup; there is but one man here who was in the ward with me at the hospital.

Suffered from hunger at Belle Isle; heard others complain; had the measles and a touch of the diarrhœa; my strength did not keep up till I got the diarrhœa; when I would go down to the river to get a drink, I could hardly stand or get back; river about fifty yards off.

My guards were not hungry, for they would sometimes throw bread in to the prisoners; have picked it up myself; it was better bread than ours; not so coarse.

I saw a man kill a dog and eat part of it, and he sold the rest of it; I got some.

his
DANIEL ⋈ McMANN.
mark.

Sworn to and subscribed before me,
May 31st, 1864.
D. P. BROWN, JR.,
United States Commissioner.

Private WALTER S. SMITH, *sworn and examined:* —

Am from New York; enlisted August 27th, 1861, in the 48th New York; captured at Morris Island, July 18th taken to Columbia, S. C.; never had any blanket; rations were corn bread—enough— small piece of meat and rice; done very well there; from there taken to Richmond — Libby Prison.

Was put on Belle Isle in two days after, tents torn, holes in them; about half of our men slept outside—fifty; it rained through the tents.

Some laid out in the snow and frost; I laid on the ground; the men that laid out, some had blankets and some had none; some froze to death; many had their feet frozen; all that slept out suffered from cold some in tents suffered from cold.

I saw men that had frozen to death in the night; I saw this seven or eight times.

We had wheat bread when we first went there; about eight inches by four and a-half, by an inch and a half or more thick; meat ration four or five times a week, as big as my three fingers, each time, for three or four months; after that got none, except once in a while; I had a chronic diarrhœa; kept my strength pretty well till then; lost flesh before.

The corn bread was very poor—ground with cob; on the days they gave us meat, they gave us less bread; when we had meat, the bread ration was about one-half the size of the loaf produced here, (same as before referred to, weighing fifteen ounces); we got half of this loaf (for the whole day) when we got meat; two-thirds when we had no meat; we never got as much as the whole loaf; when we came away, they gave us rations to last through the day—one loaf; we got soup four or five times a week at first; soup and meat same day; latter part of time, scarce any soup.

The guards fared better; they got meat when we did not; they got a third more bread; our rations not sufficient to keep down hunger; suffered the last three months; had the diarrhœa twice; got it the last time, three or four days before I came away; the men suffered very much who had been on the island for some time; felt no pain when hungry; never kept from sleeping from hunger; left Belle Isle, 17th of March; think thirty or forty died while I was there.

I have heard the men running round the tents to keep warm at all hours of the night; the river was frozen a little while I was there; the current is rapid.

The water would freeze two or three inches in the bucket at night; the main street of the camp would be very much filled with men lying there.

From the general talk from the men in the camp, I think that the statement, that seventeen men would die on an average a night, is likely to be correct.

WALTER S. SMITH.

Sworn to and subscribed before me,
May 31st, 1864.
D. P. BROWN, JR.,
United States Commissioner.

Testimony taken at United States Army General Hospital, Division No. 1, Annapolis, Maryland, June 1st, 1864.

ALL THE COMMISSIONERS PRESENT.

Private WM. W. WILCOX, of Cleveland, Ohio, *sworn and examined:*—

I enlisted August, 1862, in the 124th Ohio Volunteers.

Taken prisoner at the battle of Chickamauga, Ga., September, 1863; taken to Tunnel Hill, Ga.; was in good health at the time of capture; thence to Richmond, Va.; placed on Belle Isle.

They took everything except the natural clothing, even to knife, on body; no blankets given us; I hid my money and they did not get that.

No shelter provided; slept on bare ground; no covering in the least; was put on the Isle the last day of September, or first of October; staid there eleven days; men came when I did; had no shelter; were turned into an enclosure in which there was no shelter; I suppose there were two thousand without shelter.

Removed to the city of Richmond; we were all removed there; placed in Smith's tobacco factory; no covering nor bed until the blankets were sent to us by the United States; received the blankets about the 1st of December.

Removed to Danville, and placed in tobacco warehouse; windows broken out; miserable cold place; we took the blankets with us from Richmond; so cold, we suffered; no means to keep warm, except by walking around; the cold prevented sleeping to a great extent; a man could not sleep alone comfortable with one blanket.

There was a great deal of stealing of blankets by the guards; the men traded their blankets for rice; the guards would bring rice to the window, from fifteen to twenty pounds, and offer to exchange for our blankets; they would come to the windows and say, "stick your blanket out so I can get hold of the end of it;" then two or more of the guards would jerk the blanket away and not give the rice; this was not a general thing, though it was often done; the motive of the men for doing this, was, they were so near starved out that they were ready to take anything; the guard would pass in bags of sand in place of rice and take blankets.

When we first came there, our bread was made from middlings, shorts and bran, such as we feed our cattle; it was a combination of most everything, corn-hulls, bran, and refuse flour; got about half pound: the bulk was only one-quarter larger than the loaf shown, but was lighter than this; I should say from two to three ounces lighter.

Our beef, when we first went there, would range from four to six ounces a day.

Our soup was made from sweet potatoes; about half pint in quantity, and the liquor the beef was boiled in; some days we would not get any soup; the soup was hardly palatable.

There was a difference in our rations; we drew this black bread for about a week, then drew corn bread; the corn bread was about the size for a ration as the loaf shown here: I should judge our rations were heavier than that loaf, about two to three ounces, (loaf weighs now twelve ounces and a fraction).

In every ration there was cobs, whole corn, as hard as on the cobs, sometimes husks as long as my finger; the loaf was sweet when we first got it; not sufficient to satisfy hunger.

The way it affected me was to make me so weak I would become blind; if I'd get up to move as far as across this room, I would become blind and everything would get dark, and I would fall from weakness; my strength kept declining all the time before I got the diarrhoea; did not have much diarrhoea until the first of March.

I was removed to the hospital about the middle of December, from Danville; I had no disease I know of but weakness, swelling of the legs, with purple and inflamed and yellow spots; the skin cracked and water ran out of my legs; rations better at the hospital, when I first went there, than they were in prison; we were allowed no privilege at all in prison.

After we tunnelled out, we were only allowed to go to the privy six at a time; the floor was in one mess—filthy; an ordinary one-horse wagon load of human excrement on the floor every morning.

Not allowed to look out the window; was shot at twice for looking out; a man was shot alongside of me, while standing at the window; he was standing two feet from the window, with his hand on the casement; the sentry could not see him from the sentry's beat; I presume the sentry saw his shadow; he stepped out of his position to shoot at him, perhaps twenty to twenty-five feet; the sentry shot him in the head and killed him instantly; I suppose I have seen five hundred men shot at; our orders were not to put our heads out the windows; this man had not put his head out at that time; he had rolled up his blanket and was standing over the place where he slept on the floor; his name was Alexander Opes, of the 101st Indiana.

With one exception, we were treated very well by the physicians; never heard any fault found of any physician but Dr. Moses, of Charlestown; don't know his first name; when once we had mouldy bread given to us in the hospital, Dr. Fontleroy made a fuss about it and had it changed.

WM. W. WILCOX.

Sworn to and subscribed before me,
June 1st, 1864.
D. P. BROWN, JR.,
United States Commissioner.

Private WILLIAM D. FOOTE, recalled:—

The first case of death I remember, was a Massachusetts man, who died from frozen feet; from the looks of them you could hardly tell they were feet; he laid in the next bed to me; they first took off the toes of one of the feet, and then took off the foot; in a few days he died from amputation; he was in the same ward; brought in the middle of November. Saw no man frozen to death on Belle Isle; saw any number of men brought in with frozen feet, who afterwards suffered amputation; ten or twelve persons were so brought in; two or three of the amputated cases died; I speak of what occurred in my ward.

WILLIAM D. FOOTE.

Sworn to and subscribed before me,
June 1st, 1864.
D. P. BROWN, JR.,
United States Commissioner.

Private HIRAM J. NEAL sworn and examined:—

I am from Maine; enlisted in the 4th Maine Regiment; taken prisoner at Bristow Station, in October, 1863; taken to the Pemberton prison, from there to Belle Island, which I reached 24th February; remained until January 18th, blankets taken from me; nothing given in their place; after eight days, we had tents at Belle Island.

At first the men had to lay out till they could find tents; had nothing to sleep upon.

About one-fifth of the men were permitted by the rebels to retain their blankets; had no straw or board to lie on; tents old and rotten —full of holes; those in the tents managed to keep warm, though they couldn't sleep; those out of the tents, from three to six hundred, tried to run about to keep warm.

Saw many with frozen feet carried off; in one morning saw eleven corpses, three frozen stiff. Near first of January, deaths occurred eight or ten in twenty-four hours, principally in the night; I deem the causes of those deaths to have been exposure and starvation.

When I left, January 18th, there were about five thousand men there; I was transferred to the hospital for diarrhœa and disability.

Rations not sufficient to satisfy hunger; waked up one night and found myself gnawing my coat sleeve; used to dream of having something good to eat.

I had a pain in my chest and bowels; had the diarrhœa when I was captured; had a pain in my bowels then; had about four movements of the bowels a day before captured; not able to do duty all the time; I had been thirty-six hours on the march with one night's rest just before I was captured; was in the fight about an hour.

HIRAM J. NEAL.

Sworn to and subscribed before me,
June 1st, 1864.
D. P. BROWN, JR.,
United States Commissioner.

Private CHARLES F. PFOUNSTIEL, sworn and examined:—

I am a German; enlisted in 2d Maryland, September 24, 1862; captured in Tennessee; imprisoned in Belle Island; reached there January 21st; remained till 6th of March.

They took my blankets, sixty dollars in money, and a watch worth thirty dollars.

For two days had no shelter; then I got in the tents; air came in on every side; many men without tents; two hundred men went in with me; the greater part had no tents; some had a blanket or old coat.

Some froze to death; could not keep warm; one out of my regiment froze to death; he reported to the doctor that he was sick but he paid him no attention, perhaps because the man could not speak English.

Every morning we carried out some men froze to death, and from starvation some four or five men.

We did not get enough to eat; ten or twelve ounces of corn bread and two spoons of beans almost rotten; sometimes we had soup—not fit to eat, yet had to eat it; had meat only three or four times while I was there; two or three ounces each time; I was hungry all the time.

I could not sleep for hunger and cold, dirt and lice; I washed twice a day in the James river; strength kept up till last eight days, then I felt sick in my bowels; had no diarrhœa; did not go to the hospital; left with the 9th Maryland.

I saw a good many cases carried in a blanket to the doctor, and when they got there many of them were dead; had my feet frozen.

There might be many deaths I did not see; I have reason to believe there was. I have stated what I saw--three or four a night.

The men would dig holes in the ground to lie in at night to protect them from the air.

CHAS. F. PFOUNSTIEL.

Sworn to and subscribed before me,
June 1st, 1864.

D. P. BROWN, JR.,
United States Commissioner.

TESTIMONY OF COMMISSIONED AND MEDICAL OFFICERS.

Captain A. R. CALHOUN, *sworn and examined:*—

I am from Kentucky; was not mustered in at the time of capture; was captured at North Eastern Georgia; was taken to Libby Prison; captured in October, 1863, and reached Libby in November.

We were taken from Atlanta in open box cars, without shelter; we lay on the floor, wounded men and all; men with the diarrhœa had no accommodations, and had to perform the operations of nature in the cars; all packed closely; there was about fifty wounded; some amputations.

Just before we left Atlanta, one of our men with diarrhœa went to the back house, which was beyond the line our prisoners were allowed to go; there was a bunch of dried leaves at the corner of the back house; they could not have been a foot beyond the line, and when the man went to pick them up, the guard fired and killed him.

On entering Libby it was thirty-six hours before we had any rations given us, and would have suffered, if the officers already there had not shared with us; I mean our officers.

We were packed in a room of one hundred and forty feet long by forty-five feet wide, and already occupied by nearly three hundred men.

We had no clothing or bedding given to us; there were eleven men of us; what we had was taken from us by our captors; it was very cold; the windows were broken at each end of the room; our comrades also shared their blankets and continued to do so until we were supplied by blankets from the Sanitary Committee; even then they would not average over a blanket to a man, in my room.

It was so filthy that our clothing and blankets soon became covered with vermin; the floors of the prison were washed late in the afternoon nearly every day, so that when we came to lie down it was very damp; we had nothing but our clothing and blanket to lie on; the result was that nearly every man had a cough.

We were wormed and dove-tailed together like fish in a basket; in this room was the sink and privy; we did our washing and dried our clothes in the same room; two stoves in the room, one at each end, and two or three armfuls of wood for each per day.

We were not allowed to go within three feet of the windows to look out; but men could not help this, and were repeatedly fired upon; in this firing they wounded four officers; there was hardly a day passed without firing; any one who hung clothes near or on the windows, had the clothes confiscated and were put in the cells.

Twice each day the men were crowded into two rooms for roll call; in this room were the sick and weak who could hardly stand; the crowd was immense; our men were counted out one by one; the officers— there were one thousand officers; any one not attending this roll call was compelled to stand in ranks four hours on the floor.

When I first entered Libby in November, we received a small loaf of corn bread, about two ounces of poor beef and a little boiled rice each day; the loaf was about an inch and a half longer, thicker and heavier than this.* The crust was very thick; we used to call it iron-clad, and grate it and make mush out of it, as the most palatable way; we could not grate the crusts.

After November we received about two ounces of beef once in four weeks on an average; from the 25th of March till the 6th of May, not a bit of meat was issued in officers' quarters.

For the three months of Feburary, March, and April, there was a pint of black peas issued to each man every week, and a little vinegar; these peas were full of bugs, nearly every ration; they called them bugs, but they were little white maggots in a chrysalis state; we pounded the peas so as to mash them, and let the bugs flow to the surface; there was about an ounce of soap and a little salt given each man.

This was inadequate to satisfy hunger, and for two months I have had a burning sensation, when in prison, in my intestines. I used to dream of food, and foolishly would blame myself for not having eaten more when at home; the subject of food engrossed my entire thoughts; not all suffered as I did; the majority did; some were fortunate enough to receive boxes from home.

We were allowed to write letters once each week, not to exceed six lines.

Boxes sent us from the North were stored in a warehouse near the prison; we could see them in the windows; the contents of the boxes were being stolen or ruined by keeping, and when issued I think would have

* The same loaf before referred to.

been eaten by none but starving men; every package and can was broken open, and the contents were poured promiscuously into a blanket, so that everything ran in together; they stole a great many of our boxes: one of the guards told me that they saw our men escaping through the tunnel, and that they did not prevent them, supposing it was their own men stealing our boxes; the Sanitary supply sent us, we received but little of; we were allowed to send out and buy at extravagant prices; they sold us the Sanitary hams, butter, and stationery. Marks of the Sanitary Commission were on the cases and on the paper.

For trivial offences, officers were sent to the cells; there had been about eighty-five men in; many of those men were innocent that were placed there as hostages; they said the cells were damp, walls green, no stoves; they were about twelve feet by twenty; at one time there were sixteen men in those cells; some had to stand all night; I believe this fully. I was in the hospital with pneumonia.

Just before I left, Capt. Stevens received a small box from home, sat down and ate to excess, as any man would under the circumstances, and died a few hours afterwards.

The surgeon was very kind to us. The hospital food was just like the quarter food, with the exception of a little rye coffee and sugar; not quite so much bread.

I had a burning sensation on the inside, with a general failing in strength. A man had a piece of ham which I looked at for hours.

When I came away on the 16th of May, and saw the pale faces of the men through the bars, I cried. They begged me for God's sake to appeal to the Government and write to the papers—to do anything in the world to get them relieved. I am confident that if they remain long in that situation, they will never be fit for anything. The men never blame our Government for their suffering.

I know the Rebels have plenty, for we went down into the cellar, and brought up corn meal, flour, potatoes and turnips, which we divided with our fellows; the flour was excellent; I ate about a quart of it. I am a communicant in the church, and was studying for the ministry when the war broke out. I am a member of the Reformed Church.

A. R. CALHOUN.

Sworn to and subscribed before me,
June 1st, 1864.
D. P. BROWN, JR.,
United States Commissioner.

I certify that the foregoing testimony was taken and reduced to writing in the presence of the respective witnesses, and by them sworn to in my presence, at the times, places, and in the manner set forth.

D. P. BROWN, JR.,
United States Commissioner.

Testimony, by letter, of Lieut.-Col. Farnsworth, 1st Conn. Cavalry.

NORWICH, June 29th, 1864.

GENTLEMEN:—In reply to a letter from one of your Committee, I have the honor to make the following statement of what I saw, heard and felt of the treatment of prisoners of war by the Confederate authorities, at Richmond, Virginia:

I entered service October, 1861; was captured on the 14th of July, 1863, in a cavalry skirmish near Halltown, Va.; was conveyed to Richmond, and confined in Libby prison; was paroled and sent North on the 14th of March, 1864.

My treatment by my immediate captors was gentlemanly in the extreme; even going so far as to assist me in concealing money, so as to prevent the Richmond authorities from robbing me.

Upon reaching the Libby, we were rigidly searched, and all moneys and attractive jack-knives, nice overcoats and meerschaum pipes were kindly appropriated by the prison authorities; rubber blankets, canteens, spurs and haversacks were taken from us. Lieut. Moran, for complaining of this treatment, was knocked down by Richard Turner, inspector of the prison clothing.

There was never an issue of clothing or blankets made by the Confederate authorities during the time I was there confined. We did receive one hundred (100) each of tin plates, cups, knives, forks, (mostly damaged by bayonet-thrusts, they having been picked up from battle-fields), for the use of one thousand (1000) officers.

ACCOMMODATIONS—In six (6) rooms, one hundred by forty, there were confined as many as twelve hundred (1200) officers of all ranks, from Brigadier-General to Second Lieutenant. This space was all that was allowed us in which to cook, eat, wash, sleep and exercise. You can see that soldierly muscle must fast deteriorate when confined to twenty (20) superficial feet of plank; we were not allowed benches, chairs or stools, nor even to fold our blankets and sit upon them; but were forced to sit like so many slaves upon the middle passage.

This continued until the appointment of General Butler, Commissioner of Exchange, after which time we were allowed chairs and stools, which we made from the boxes and barrels sent us from the North.

There was plenty of water allowed us, and a tank for bathing in four (4) of the rooms.

There were seventy-six (76) windows in the six (6) rooms, from which in winter there was no protection.

SUBSISTENCE.—Our rations consisted of one-quarter (¼) of a pound of beef, nine (9) ounces of bread of variable quality, generally of wheat flour. Although sometimes of weat flour and corn meal, a gill of rice, and a modicum of salt and vinegar per day. This continued until the 11th of November, which was the first day that meat was not issued, and bread made entirely of corn meal was substituted for wheat bread; this meal was composed of cob and grain ground together, and when mixed with cold water, without salt or any raising, made the bread. Meat was next issued on the 14th, and the issue suspended on the 21st. On the 26th we received salt pork, sent to the prisoners by the United States Government; from this time out, meat was like angels' visits; sometimes it was issued at intervals of ten days, and sometimes not in thirty (30); the longest interval was thirty-four (34) days.

The amount of rations first issued will undoubtedly sustain life; but their long continuance without exercise will produce disease of a scorbutic nature.

The rations issued after the 11th of November will not sustain life, and without the aid sent to us from the North the mortality would have been great. Nine ounces of such corn bread and a cup of water per day, are poorer rations than those issued to the vilest criminal in the meanest States prison in the Union; yet this was considered fit treatment by the *hospitable* chivalry of the South to be extended to men taken in honorable warfare, any one of them the peer of the arch traitor, Jeff. Davis.

BOXES.—We began to receive boxes in October. These came in good order, were inspected in our presence, and delivered to us entire; they came regularly, and were delivered in good order up to about the first of January; after this time boxes were sent regularly from the North, and were received by Col. Ould, Commissioner of Exchange, but they were *not* issued to us; they were stored in a building within sight of the prison, and at the time of my leaving, three thousand (3000) had been received there and not delivered to us; what was the cause of this non-delivery of boxes we were never informed. They keep up a semblance of delivery, however, by the issue of five (5) or six (6) a week, they receiving from the North about three hundred (300) a week.

The contents of these boxes were, undoubtedly, appropriated to the private use of the officials in and about Richmond. Here is simply one instance: Lieut. Maginnis, of the 18th Reg., Conn., since killed in battle, recognized a suit of citizen's clothes which had been sent to him from the North, on the person of one of the prison officials, and accused him of the theft, and showed his name on the watch pocket of the pants. Such cases were numerous.

BELLE ISLE.—Upon the 26th day of January, 1864, I visited Belle Island, as an assistant in the distribution of clothing sent by the Government, and by the Sanitary Commissions of the North; this was my first time outside of the prison walls in six months. The island is situated just opposite the Tredegar Iron Works in the James river. The space occupied by prisoners is about six acres, enclosed by an earthwork three (3) feet in height; within this space were confined as many as ten thousand (10,000) prisoners. The part occupied by the prisoners is a low, sandy, barren waste, exposed in summer to a burning sun, without the shadow of a single tree; and in winter, to the damp and cold winds up the river, with a few miserable tents, in which, perhaps, one-half (½) the number were protected from the night fogs of a malarious region; the others lay upon the ground in the open air. One of them said to me: "We lay in rows, like hogs in winter, and take turns who has the outside of the row."

In the morning, the row of the previous night was plainly marked by the bodies of those who were sleeping on in their last sleep.

Fed upon corn bread and water, scantily clothed, with but few blankets, our patriotic soldiers here suffered the severest misfortunes of this war. Here, by hundreds, they offered up their lives in their country's cause, victims of disease, starvation and exposure,—sufferings a thousand times more dreadful than the wounds of the battle-field. As many as fourteen (14) have been known to freeze to death in one night. This I have from men of my own regiment, and it is perfectly reliable.

The hospitals upon the island are Sibley tents, without floors, the ground covered with straw, and logs of wood placed around for pillows, to which, when about to die, he men were carried; and here, with logs for their pillows, the hard, cold ground for their bed, death came to their relief, and the grave closed over the victims of rebel barbarity.

The officer in charge of the island was well spoken of by the men. He deprecated the condition they were in, but said he could do no more, for the authorities gave him no more to do with; and yet it is a fact that the men were stimulated to work at their trades, as blacksmiths, etc., for the benefit of the Confederate Government, by the offer of double the quantity of rations they were then receiving; thus acting out, in their treatment of Northern soldiers, the great principle of Slavery and of the South, that the lives of the poor and helpless are in their eyes of no more value than the amount of interest they will produce on capital.

The facilities for washing were good, a sandy beach all around the island, and the whole number of prisoners could have washed in the course of the day; but, under the management of the authorities, only a limited number (say 75 men per day) were able to wash, being conducted under guard to the water, in squads of five (5) or six (6).

The sickness caused by the above treatment was of the respiratory organs, pneumonia, &c., and chronic diarrhœa.

Men were without medical treatment on the island until disease was so far advanced that when taken away in ambulances to the hospital, in squads of twenty (20), one-half ($\frac{1}{2}$) of them have died within five (5) hours — some of them while their names were being taken at the hospital.

Men were returned from the hospital to the island when so weak that they have been obliged to crawl upon their hands and knees a part of the way.

On the 20th of November, 1863, a squad were passing the prison (Libby) in this condition, going from the hospital to the island; among them was George Ward, a schoolmate of mine and of Col. Ely, of the 18th Conn. Vols. Col. Ely threw a ham to him from the window. As the poor fellow crawled to get it, the rebel guard charged bayonets on him, called him a damned Yankee, and appropriated the ham.

The bodies of the dead were placed in the cellar of the prison, to which there was free access for animals from the street. I have known of bodies being partially devoured by dogs, and hogs, and rats, during the night. Every morning the bodies were placed in rude coffins and taken away for burial. Officers have marked the coffins thus taken away, and have seen them returned twenty (20) times for bodies. You may draw your own inference as to the rites of burial extended to a Yankee prisoner in the Capital of the Southern Confederacy.

Officers dying, their brother officers procured metallic coffins and a vault, in which they were placed until they could be removed North. An officer, (Major Morris, of the 6th Pennsylvania Cavalry, I think,) who had in the hands of the Confederate authorities several hundred dollars, taken from him when he entered the prison, died in the hospital, and the authorities refused to use his money for a decent burial, and we raised it in the prison.

LIBBY MINED.— Upon the approach of Kilpatrick on his grand raid on Richmond, about the 1st March, the greatest consternation was produced among the inhabitants. The authorities felt sure of his ability to enter the city and free the prisoners.

We were informed one morning by the negroes who labor around the prison, that during the night they had been engaged in excavating a large hole under the centre of the building, and that a quantity of powder had been placed therein. Upon inquiring of certain of the guards, we found it the general impression among them that the prison was mined.

Richard Turner, inspector of the prison, told officers there confined, that "should Kilpatrick succeed in entering Richmond, it would not help us, as the prison authorities would blow up the prison and all its inmates."

The adjutant of the prison, Lieutenant Latouche, was heard by an officer (Lieutenant Jones, 55th Ohio) to use the following words to a rebel officer with whom he had entered and examined the cellar where the powder was reported as placed: "There is enough there to send every damned Yankee to hell."

Major Turner said in my presence the day we were paroled, in answer to the question, "Was the prison mined?" "Yes, and I would have blown you all to Hades before I would have suffered you to be rescued."

Bishop Johns said in the prison, when asked if he thought it was a Christian mode of warfare to blow up defenceless prisoners: "He supposed the authorities were satisfied on that point, though he did not mean to justify it."

I am very respectfully,
Your obedient servant,
CHAS. FARNSWORTH.
Late Lieutenant-Colonel 1st Connecticut Cavalry.

NORWICH, June 30th, 1864.
STATE OF CONNECTICUT, }
County of New London, }

Personally appeared CHARLES FARNSWORTH, signer of the foregoing instrument and statement, and made solemn oath that the facts stated therein are true, before me.
DAVID YOUNG,
Justice of the Peace.

Additional Testimony by Letter of Lieutenant-Colonel Farnsworth.

NORWICH, CONN., July 16th, 1864.

REV. TREADWELL WALDEN, Philadelphia:

SIR:— Your favor of the 14th inst. received. In answer to your request for a written statement of facts, related to you by myself in conversation, in regard to the conduct of the guards at Richmond, Virginia, and the provision made for the sick upon Belle Isle, I submit the following:

In what is known as the "Pemberton buildings," nearly opposite the "Libby," there were confined a large number of enlisted men. Hardly a day went by that the guards did not fire upon the prisoners. I have known as many as fourteen shots to be fired in one day. They were thus subject to death if they merely came near the window to obtain fresh air. It was a very common occurrence to hear the report of a musket and then see the sergeant of the guard bring out a wounded or dead soldier.

The guards would watch for an opportunity to fire upon their prisoners, and, without warning the prisoner to leave the vicinity of the window, fire.

Lieutenant Hammond, of the Ringgold cavalry, (better known to Libbians as "Old Imboden,") was at the sink, which is constructed upon the outside of the building. From the upper part of the sides, boards are removed for the purpose of light or ventilation. The guard below caught sight of Lieutenant Hammond's hat, through this opening, and fired. The ball entered the side, far below the opening, showing that the guard was intent upon striking his man; but a nail gave the bullet an upward turn and it passed through Hammond's ear and hat-brim. From the position he was in, there is little doubt that but for the ball striking the nail he would have been struck in the breast.

The attention of Major Turner was called to it, but he only laughed and said, "The boys were in want of practice." The guard, when spoken to about it, said "He had made a bet that he would kill a damned Yankee before he came off guard." There was not the least attention paid by the commander of the Libby prison to this deliberate attempt at *murder*.

Lieutenant Thomas Huggins, of a New York regiment, was standing at least eight feet from a window on the second floor; the guard could just see the top of his hat. To be sure of his man, the guard left his beat and stepped into the street. Being seen, a warning cry was uttered, and Huggins stooped and the bullet buried itself in the beams above. This was the same guard that fired at Hammond.

Richard, or as usually called, Dick Turner was the inspector of the prison, and acted under the orders of the commander. There was nothing too mean for him to do. He searched you when you entered, knocked you down if you grumbled, took your blanket from you if found lying upon it after morning roll-call, never spoke of you except as damned Yankees — told you "yo₃ were better treated than you deserved."

This "high-toned Southron" was employed as the negro-whipper of the prison.

Colonel Powell, 2d Virginia cavalry, (Union,) Colonel Streight and Captain Reed, 51st Indiana, and others who had been confined in the cells, used to witness the whippings, (the cells were at one end of the cellar where the whipping-block was,) and they could hear, — even if they shut their eyes to the horrid exhibition.

Colonels Powell and Streight told me of as many as six negro women having been stripped and whipped, at one time, for having passed bread to our soldiers as they marched through the street.

The flogging of the negroes that worked at the Libby was an every-day occurrence.

These blacks were free negroes from the North, who were employed as servants, but fell into the hands of the enemy. He flogged one of them so severely that he was unable to move for two weeks, and walked lame months after. His offence was resisting a white negro-driver.

The hospital tents on Belle Isle were old Sibleys. These were not temporary hospitals, for many died in them each day; but when they could not contain all the sick some sick were removed to Richmond hospitals. These tents were awful places for human beings to be placed in — without floors, a heap of straw for a bed, logs of wood for pillows — men died with less attention than many a man pays to a favorite dog. The hospitals in Richmond were much better, being in buildings, and were furnished with bunks and straw beds — some of them with sheets. But though treated with kindness, compared with Belle Island, the want of proper medicines was visible, and many died for the want of the most simple remedies.

Upon the 25th of October, 1863, two officers, (Major Hewsten, 132d New York, and a Lieutenant 4th New York Cavalry,) escaped from the hospital. Immediately, upon its being known, all the sick who were well enough to sit up or stand, were removed from the room and placed in an empty room under our prison. Here they were kept for twenty-four hours, without food or blankets, as a punishment, it was said, for not reporting the contemplated escape of the officers named. From this treatment, Surgeon Pierce of the 5th Maryland died.

The officers in the room above, removed a portion of the floor and furnished the sick with food and drink, and shared their blankets with them. This coming to the knowledge of Major Turner, we were deprived of rations for one day — October 29th, 1863.

This was not the action of the surgeons of the Libby, for, with one exception, they were kind and attentive, and did all in their power for our comfort, but of the commander of the department, Brigadier-General Winder, and of Major Turner, commander of the prison, who, I am informed, was dismissed from West Point, by orders from the Secretary of War, having been convicted of forgery.

I was informed by men whom I knew — Ward and Winship of the 18th Connecticut and Ferris and Stone of the 1st Connecticut — that the enclosure in Belle Isle was a mass of filth every morning, from the inability of the men to proceed to the sinks after evening.

Many of the guards would fire upon the prisoners for the least violation of the rules. The men were in a miserable condition and looked sickly, worn out — starvation and exposure was expressed upon their features.

Trusting that the above will assist you in your report,

I am respectfully yours,
CHARLES FARNSWORTH.

Sworn to and subscribed before me, this 18th day, of July, A. D. 1864.
DAVID YOUNG,
Justice of the Peace.

Testimony taken at Washington, D. C., June 2d, 1864.

COMMISSIONERS PRESENT.—Mr. Wilkins, Dr. Wallace, Mr. Walden.

Surgeon Nelson D. Ferguson, *sworn and examined:*—

Surgeon 8th New York Cavalry; residence, Jefferson county, N. Y.; captured 12th May, 1863; taken to Libby Prison same day; remained there twelve days; found Union officers there; my treatment same as officers received; daily rations, when first entered, were four inches by four inches by two of unbolted bread, which was coarse and sour about half the time; a ration of beans, worm-eaten, once a day; about seven quarts to fifty-three or fifty-four men, or a gill to each man was served; no other food was furnished by the Confederates; what other they had was bought with their own money.

(The ration of light bread of a common soldier in the United States Army is twenty-two ounces, and twelve ounces of pork or twenty of beef; besides that, our soldiers have thirty pound of potatoes for one hundred rations, or nearly a third of a pound per day to each man, besides coffee and sugar, &c., &c.)

The food furnished us was insufficient for healthful support of life.

When I reached the Libby Prison there were say twenty-five Union officers, no more, in the prison, recently captured; all the former occupants had been removed, as I am informed (and believe) by the rebels, to the number of seven hundred or over; when I left the prison on the 28th, there were sixty-nine Union officers there.

I spent four days in Hospital No. 21, where *wounded* Union prisoners (very few *sick*) were under treatment; I was there partly as a visitor, and also did partial duty as a surgeon in the ward; I was too ill to do full duty; I had better rations in the hospital than in prison, for I had rye coffee and a little meat, say two ounces daily, very poor bacon; the wounded men had the same ration of bread, no beans, two ounces of meat, rye coffee, occasionally a little sugar, and one gallon milk and one gallon whiskey, divided among two hundred and sixty men, or about a tablespoonful of whiskey and milk per man; they had no other nutriment or stimulation.

I consider the nourishment and stimulation they received entirely insufficient to give them a proper chance for recovery. I am surprised that more do not die. There were many bad cases among them that must inevitably sink under this treatment after a few days, and therefore I cannot state the true proportion of deaths. The condition of these men was such that any medical observer would impute it to insufficient stimulation and nutrition. The condition of the wounds generally was very unhealthy, not tending to heal, pale and flabby, and the tissues lax — just such a condition as we expect to see where the patient is improperly nourished by deficient nutrition. These wounded have all been brought there since the battle of Spottsylvania Court House.

When I was captured, I was brought into a rebel fort. It was raining. I had on a rubber blanket; the blanket was taken from my shoulders by a lieutenant, by the authority and consent of the commanding officer. I remonstrated against his taking my private property, and appealed to the commanding officer for protection, and to protect my rights. He replied, " Damn you, you have no rights." It was not possible for him to have been ignorant of the fact that I was a medical officer. Some two or three hours afterwards, when I was about to leave the fort for Libby Prison, the lieutenant remarked to me, " I hope I have treated you kindly." I replied, " I have always treated your men and officers with kindness and consideration, but you have treated me harshly." I don't think he made any reply. The Provost-Marshal took away my sabre. I told him it was my private property, and that he ought not to take it away, and his answer was, " It don't make any difference, I have a friend to whom I intend to give it."

I have had wounded rebels under my hand for treatment on various occasions. The course I have always adopted is, to take care of my own men first, then the rebels, giving them equal care and attention of every kind. I have taken my own private rations and given them repeatedly to wounded rebels. All other medical officers of our army have done likewise, as far as my observation has extended.

I have been in the service two years and eight months, and I have been in all the cavalry fights of the Army of the Potomac since I entered the service.

The buildings in Richmond occupied for hospital purposes are well suited for such purposes, being large, convenient, and well ventilated. The wards are well supplied with water, and tolerably cleanly. The prison (Libby) had just been thoroughly cleaned and was well white-washed. In the prison, we had one blanket as bed, and one as cover.

No one can appreciate, without experience, the condition of the officers in the prison during the twelve days of my stay. Their faces were pinched with hunger. I have seen an officer, standing by the window, gnawing a bone like a dog. I asked him "what do you do it for?" His reply was, "It will help fill up." They were constantly complaining of hunger. There was a sad and insatiable expression of the face impossible to describe.

The bedding in Hospital No. 21, where the privates were confined by wounds, was very dirty. The covering was entirely old dirty quilts. The beds were offensive from the discharges from wounds and secretion of the body, and were utterly unfit to place a sick or wounded man on. On the faces of the wounded there was an anxious, haggard expression of countenance, such as I have never seen before. I attribute it to want of care, want of nourishment and encouragement. There is a deficiency of medical supplies, such as bandages, lint, sticking-plaster, and medicines generally in this hospital, whether from actual want of these articles, or from unwillingness to supply them, I do not know.

N. D. FURGUSON,
Surgeon 8th N. Y. Cavalry

Sworn and subscribed before me, at Washington, D. C., this 3d day of June, A. D. 1864.
M. H. KENDIG,
Notary Public.

D. W. Richards, M. D., *sworn and examined:*—

Residence, Northampton County, Pa.; employment, Assistant Surgeon in 145th Pennsylvania Volunteers; taken prisoner May 10th, 1863; conveyed to Prison Hospital No. 21, in Richmond, on the 20th of May, and left there 28th May.

I have heard Dr. Furguson's deposition, as made before this Committee. I corroborate that testimony as relating to the condition and treatment of wounded prisoners. I know nothing further in regard to this matter.

D. W. RICHARDS,
Assistant Surgeon 145th P. V.

Sworn and subscribed before me, at Washington, D. C., this 3d day of June, A. D. 1864.
M. H. N. KENDIG,
Notary Public.

EVIDENCE OF UNITED STATES ARMY SURGEONS, IN CHARGE OF THE FOUR HOSPITALS AT ANNAPOLIS AND BALTIMORE, MD., TO WHICH RETURNED UNION PRISONERS WERE BROUGHT FROM RICHMOND, VA.

ALSO, EVIDENCE OBTAINED FROM EYE-WITNESSES.

Testimony of Surgeon B. A. VanderKieft, in charge of United States Army General Hospital Division No. 1, Annapolis, Maryland. Taken at the Hospital, May 31st, 1864.

COMMISSIONERS PRESENT.—Mr. Wilkins, Dr. Wallace, Mr. Walden.

I have been the recipient of all the prisoners returned from Richmond since the 1st of June, 1863, except one steamboat load which were four hundred to five hundred. I have received, I should judge, nearly (3000) three thousand; these are in a debilitated condition, badly clad, and down-spirited, on account of ill-treatment by starvation and exposure, as they all on inquiry agree in stating, and as I am convinced is the case by their actual condition on their arrival, and by rations shown to me, which they unanimously state are the only ones given them.

They unanimously state that their blankets, overcoats, watches, and jewelry and money have been taken from them, partially by their immediate captors, but also in a quasi-official way, telling them that they will be restored when they are released, which, as far as I know, and have been informed, have never been done.

The returned prisoners state that the officials, such as guards and nurses, often receive money from them, such as they may have been able to secrete, with the promise that they shall have the equivalent returned in food, which promise is not performed.

Colonel Palmer de Cesnola (4th New York Cavalry) told me that while acting as distributing commissary of articles of food and clothing sent by United States Government and United States Sanitary Commission, he observed that some of our prisoners at Richmond and Belle Isle, in order to receive a less cruel treatment and to obtain larger rations, were acting as shoemakers for the Rebel Government. He at once told those men that such action was disloyal, as by so doing they indirectly assisted the rebellion. The result of this remark induced the rebel authorities to deprive him of the privilege of being longer a distributing commissary.

Almost in all cases I find that our men state that when they were captured, they were in very good condition as to general physical health; but I do not even need such a statement, as I am well acquainted with the regulations which govern the medical department of our army, "to send to the rear every man who is not perfectly able to bear arms," and if a few feeble men have fallen into the hands of the rebels, they belong to the class called "stragglers," which certainly belong to the minority.

From my experience of fifteen years of constant medical and military service in Northern Europe, the East Indies, and Mediterranean, as well as in our own army since September, 1861, I affirm that the treatment to which our men have been subjected while prisoners of war in the hands of the enemy, is against all rules of civilized warfare, and that I would prefer to fall into the hands of the Chinese of Borneo, called "Anack Baba," who murder their prisoners, than to fall into the hands of the rebels, where the lives and comfort of prisoners of war is a matter of such cruel indifference, to say the least, if not indeed, as one might almost be justified in supposing, a matter of determined policy.

If I may believe the statements of our returned prisoners, the diseases under which they are suffering when they come into my hands, are attributable to the following causes, one or more: deprivation of clothing, deficiency of food in quantity and quality, want of fresh air, on account of overcrowding in prison buildings and consequent unavoidable uncleanliness, and mental depression, the result of the above causes, and want of adequate shelter, exposure during the fall and winter.

The diseases most common among these returned prisoners are scurvy, diarrhœa, and congestion of the lungs, which are not amenable to the ordinary treatment in use in civil life or in hospitals of our own army.

They are most successfully mastered by high nutrition and stimulation, with cleanliness and fresh air — medicinal treatment being of small assistance in the recovery of the sufferers, and often being entirely dispensed with.

The medical records in my office show that this system is the only valid and effective mode of management, thus proving by the counteracting effect of good food, air, cleanliness, and stimulants, that these disorders are the result of the causes above stated.

I swear the above statement to be true.

B. A. VANDERKIEFT,
Surgeon U. S. Volunteers in Charge.

Sworn and subscribed before me, this sixth day of June, in the year of our Lord one thousand eight hundred and sixty-four, (June 6th, 1864.)

[SEAL.]   H. P. LESLIE,
Notary Public for and in the County of Anne Arundel, Maryland.

Testimony, by Letter, of Surgeon William S. Ely, Executive Officer U. S. A. General Hospital Division, No. 1, Annapolis, Maryland, June 6th, 1864.

Dr. ELLERSLIE WALLACE, Philadelphia, Penn.

DOCTOR:— I am in receipt of your communication of the 2nd inst., and would reply as follows:—

I am an Assistant Surgeon of Volunteers in the service of the United States, and have been on duty in this hospital since October 3d, 1863, as executive officer and medical officer in charge of a ward. I have been present on the arrival of nearly every boatload of paroled prisoners since my connection with this hospital commenced.

I remember distinctly the arrival of the flag-of-truce steamer "New York," November 18th, 1863, and was present and assisted in unloading the men. I went on board the boat and saw bodies of six (6) men who had died during the passage of the steamer from City Point, Va., to this place. No words can describe their appearance. In each case the sunken eye, the gaping mouth, the filthy skin, the clothes and head alive with vermin, the repelling, bony contour — all conspired to lead to the conclusion that we were looking upon the victims of starvation, cruelty and exposure, to a degree unparalleled in the history of humanity.

I have never seen more than the above number of dead in any single arrival; but at other dates, and on several occasions, I have seen two (2) and three (3) dead on board the boat, and have repeatedly known four (4) or six (6) to die within twelve (12) hours of their reception into hospital. The same condition evidenced in the cases of the six (6) referred to above, has characterized nearly every instance, and leads us irresistibly to the conclusion that death has been owing to a long series of exposure and hardships, with a deprivation of the barest necessities for existence.

I have known paroled prisoners of war to be admitted to this hospital with barely sufficient clothing to cover their nakedness. I cannot say that I have seen any single case where a patient was admitted without *either* hat, coat, shoes, shirt, or stockings, but I have repeatedly seen men without one (1), two (2), or three (3) of these articles, and think that I can say, that when they possessed all, it was an exceptional case. It is our *rule* to strip each patient to his skin, and provide all with entirely new clothing, because rags, filth and vermin preponderate so largely as to render any further use of the various articles of apparel upon the bodies of patients reaching this point from Richmond, Va., unhealthy, and in opposition to the simplest principles of hygiene.

Patients, when asked the manner in which they lost their clothing, reply that they were robbed of what they had when captured, or else, that during their imprisonment, oftentimes extending over many months, their clothing, piece by piece, wore out, and that they had no opportunity to procure a change.

It is impossible for any, save those who have seen the condition of paroled men soon after their release from captivity, to have any idea of the *state of the skin* covering their bodies. In many cases that I have observed, the dirt incrustation has been so thick as to require months of constant ablution to recover the normal condition and function of the integument. Patients have repeatedly stated, in answer to my interrogations, "that they had been unable to wash their bodies once in *six* (6) *months;*" that all that time they had lain in the dirt, and, as might naturally be expected, the filth accumulation was constantly increasing. Frequently, the entire cuticle must die and be detached before any healthy action can be recovered.

I know not how to better compare the cutaneous condition of these men in its different morbid states, than to liken it, in feeling, to the effect produced upon the fingers by passing them over sand-paper from the coarsest quality down to that moderately fine.

Diaphoretic action in many such cases, I have found almost unattainable. When we consider the importance of the cutaneous secretion, relative to a state of health, it cannot be denied that, in many instances under attention, this is the prime exciting cause of the diseases of the pulmonary and abdominal organs, which are so constantly found among our Richmond patients.

A great many post-mortem examinations of paroled prisoners who have died in our hospitals, have been made by myself and others. The thoracic organs are seldom found healthy. The pectoral muscles are so much wasted as to render the walls of the chest, to a certain extent, transparent. The lungs frequently are found filling but half the pulmonary cavities. Old pleuritic adhesions, in all degrees of extent, are generally seen; almost invariably there is a local stasis or congestion of blood, posteriorly and about the roots of the lungs: the heart is found flaccid, and often its walls are attenuated; when taken out and laid down, it flattens from its own weight, is seldom filled with a substantial clot, and generally contains but a very little dark, thin blood. Tubercular deposit is sometimes very extensive, and in cases where there is no external appearance favoring the scrofulous diathesis, leading me to the conclusion that it has been engendered ofttimes, in a previously healthy subject, by the deprivation of good, wholesome food, and the combination of unhealthy influences, to which so many of our prisoners of war succumb. The liver is unusually pale in color, and of anæmic aspect; the intestines are sometimes much diseased, but frequently healthy. I have known many instances of marked *chronic diarrhœa,* resulting fatally, yet disclosing no *organic* intestinal changes or morbid appearances,— favoring the supposition that the diarrhœa is often only a *symptom* of a want of tonicity, not of organic disease.

I consider the frequency of pulmonary congestions among our patients from Richmond owing to the altered condition of the fluids of the system, especially the blood: its fibrinous portion becomes diminished, and stagnation takes place in the most depending portions of the lungs, giving us what we term a *hypostatic pneumonia,* depending on the want of tone in the vessels and consequent enfeebled circulation.

The treatment which I have found most effective in aiding the restoration to health of our reduced Richmond patients, is, very briefly, as follows:— Quinine, iron, and cod-liver oil, (in their different preparations and combinations), in *small* doses; liquid concentrated nourishment, a rigid enforcement of cleanliness, and regularity in eating and drinking, and, if possible, the hygienic advantages of a *tent* ward.

Our records exhibit a mortality among our patients from Richmond of 18 per cent.

I am, Doctor, very respectfully,
Your obedient servant,
WILLIAM S. ELY,
Assistant Surgeon U. S. Volunteers.

Personally appeared before me this sixth day of June, 1864, William S. Ely, Assistant Surgeon U. S. Volunteers, and took oath that the statements above made are true to the best of his knowledge and belief.

[SEAL.] HENRY P. LESLIE,
Notary Public, Anne Arundel Co., Md.

Testimony of Surgeon G. B. Parker, in charge of United States Army General Hospital, Division No. 2, Annapolis, Maryland. Taken at the Hospital, May 31st, 1864.

ALL THE COMMISSIONERS PRESENT.

Surgeon G. B. PARKER, *sworn and examined:* —

I have been in charge of this hospital one year. During this time I have received a large number of prisoners in exchange. Their condition has been very low, very feeble, since last June. The large proportion of the cases received here are marked "Debilitas." It was not specific disease with them; where it was, it was coupled with debility.

The majority of the diseased cases were diarrhœa caused by bad diet — of insufficient and bad quality; they have resulted from the want of variety of diet. This will produce scurvy.

I have seen an hundred of the rations served to the men. I do not consider the rations I have seen sufficient for the support of life for any long time.

We give our men twenty ounces of beef on a march, per day, and twenty-two ounces of bread. Fourteen ounces of meat and ten ounces of bread will keep any man from starving; less than twelve ounces of bread and ten ounces of meat per diem would produce disease, and, if long continued, would fail to keep life up to the standard in a great majority of men. Lower than this would end in debility and decline; in proportion as you vary a man's diet, so is his general health.*

The majority of the men did walk from the landing here. We did not receive the worst cases. In the main, the diseases were produced by insufficient and a bad quality of diet. Their stomachs were not able to retain a sufficient quantity of solid food when the men first got here. I was led to the belief that the diarrhœa was produced by bad diet.

I found nutrition was the most successful treatment.

Have had cases of frost bite here resulting in mortification of the ends of the toes. Those were cases from Richmond — eight or ten cases.

Though the men would be strong enough to walk from the dock up here, at the same time they were in that debilitated condition that a slight change of air would cause congestion of the lungs, and death. Stimulants and tonics are largely used.

There were a good many cases of scurvy. In the majority of cases of diarrhœa, there would be scorbutic symptoms. I had at one time eight returned prisoners who lost their teeth. I suppose this was owing to the treatment these men had received, and their diet.

At the hospital we give each man twenty ounces of bread per day, and one pound of meat, including bone; could not give the percentage of bone; we also give vegetables. In the winter we give cabbage, potatoes, rice and beans, molasses, tea, butter. A healthy soldier would get no butter. Twelve ounces of meat and twelve ounces of bread per day, rejecting the other articles, would be insufficient to preserve good health.

G. B. PARKER.

Sworn to and subscribed before me,
May 31st, 1864.
D. P. BROWN, JR.,
United States Commissioner.

JUNE 1st, 1864.

COMMISSIONER PRESENT. — Hon. J. L Clark Hare.

Surgeon G. B. PARKER, *who was before sworn, recalled:* —

A great many of those whom I mentioned yesterday as suffering from debility and no specific disease, afterwards recovered. Several cases where their appearance was really favorable died very suddenly. On examination, post mortem, they were found exsanguinated to a wonderful degree; the evidence of which was in large white fibrinous clots in the left side of the heart, and extending into the aorta. This was found to be the case with the majority of those who died. In other cases, as I mentioned yesterday, they would take on acute disease, generally congestion of the lungs, and die within twenty-four hours after the attack.

G. B. PARKER,
Assistant Surgeon U. S. Army.

---

* A ration which had been given to one of the men, produced and weighed: — weight two ounces of bread, and three-sixteenths of an ounce of meat in its dry state

Testimony of Surgeon De Witt C. Peters, in charge of Jarvis General Hospital, Baltimore, Md., taken at Baltimore June 1st, 1864.

COMMISSIONERS PRESENT:—Dr. Mott, Dr. Delafield, Judge Hare.

DE WITT C. PETERS, *sworn and examined:*—

I am an Assistant-Surgeon of the United States Army, stationed at Jarvis General Hospital, Baltimore. On or about the 16th of April, 1864, I received at the hospital over which I had charge, some two hundred and fifty paroled prisoners of war, recently returned from Belle Island and Richmond.

The greater majority of these men were in a semi-state of nudity. They were laboring under such diseases as chronic diarrhœa, phthisis pulmonalis, scurvy, frost bites, general debility, caused by starvation, neglect, and exposure. Many of them had partially lost their reason, forgetting even the date of their capture and every thing connected with their antecedent history. They resemble, in many respects, patients laboring under cretinism.

They were filthy in the extreme, covered with vermin. Some had extensive bed sores caused by laying in the sand and dirt, and nearly all were extremely emaciated; so much so that they had to be cared for even like infants. Their hair had not been cut, nor the men shaved in many instances for months. On inquiry of these men as to what was the matter with them, the invariable answer was starvation, exposure, and neglect, while prisoners on Belle Island. They informed me, that while on Belle Island during the inclement months of the past winter, there were congregated at one time in a space less than three acres, one hundred and ten squads of prisoners, each numbering one hundred persons. Less than half of these had old worn-out Sibley and other tents for shelter. The remainder were obliged to accommodate themselves as best they could. But a few of them had blankets. These were issued to them by our Government under flag of truce. Some had overcoats. Many had no shoes except patches that they had contrived themselves.

Those that escaped freezing to death during the cold nights, did so by exercising and by huddling together in heaps like hogs, alternating places with those more exposed in the heaps, and with those in the tents, until at last they were obliged to go to the hospital.

They informed me, that each morning, numbers were found frozen to death, who had probably died from other causes—exhaustion. They stated to me further, that they believed this system of slow starvation was carried on to prevent other men from enlisting in our army.

The ration allowed them was a small piece of corn bread, the meal of which contained also the cob, a little rice soup very rarely, and sometimes, but rarely, a small quantity of meat—a few ounces; they confessed that they had eaten dog meat whenever they were so fortunate as to capture a dog.

In the hospitals, according to the statement made to me by Hospital Steward James, United States Army, they fared a little better, although, even there, they had an insufficiency of food, and the beds were filthy and covered with vermin. He states that at hospital No. 21, where he was serving as one of the apothecaries during three months, January, February and March, there were admitted two thousand seven hundred of our men, of whom nearly fourteen hundred and fifty died.* They lacked medicines and all appliances needed for the sick. The patients in the hospital had one advantage over prisoners of war on Belle Island: that was, they were allowed to buy a loaf of bread the size of a man's fist, for which they paid five or six dollars Confederate money.

Out of the two hundred and fifty men received by me, so far, fifteen have died; the post-mortems of which have made apparent diseases of nearly all the viscera to a remarkable extent.

I received one man incurably insane, caused, as I was informed and believe, by joy, produced by the news that he was to be exchanged. I found, from excess of habit, they had become like savages in their habits, and lost the decencies of life, and had to be taught like children the decencies of society.

The health and constitutions of the majority of these men are permanently undermined. Under proper care and treatment, which consisted in their not eating too much, a spare but concentrated diet, may have rallied. In one instance a boy gained forty pounds in two weeks; he still has phthisis and can hardly stand exposure or active exercise. A case of scurvy occurred among others which is the worst I ever saw or read of; a man turning red or nearly black from head to foot; he died in twenty-four hours.

I think nine-tenths of the men weighed under one hundred pounds; they appeared to be articulated skeletons; covered with simply integument; had dropsy and œdema

---

* The quarterly report from which these figures are taken, was obtained and brought home by a returned Union prisoner. It will be found on pages 68—9.

in the feet, caused by weakness; and were the most pitiable objects to behold. They had an uncontrollable appetite.

DE WITT C. PETERS,
Assist. Surgeon United States Army, in charge of Jarvis Hospital, Baltimore, Md.

Sworn to and subscribed before me,
June 1st, 1864.
D. P. BROWN, JR.,
United States Commissioner.

Testimony of Surgeon A. Chapel, in charge of West's Buildings Hospital, Baltimore, Md., taken at Baltimore, June 2, 1864.

COMMISSIONERS PRESENT:— Dr. Mott, Dr. Delafield, Judge Hare.

Surgeon A. CHAPEL, *affirmed and examined*:—

I am Surgeon in charge of West's Buildings Hospital, Baltimore. On the 18th of April, 1864, I received at the hospital one hundred and five of the paroled prisoners from Richmond, brought to this point on the flag-of-truce boat "New York." These were the worst cases received at this point by that boat; none of them being able to stand alone. All were brought into the hospital upon stretchers.

Nearly all were in an extreme state of emaciation. filthy in the extreme, and covered with vermin. Some of them so eaten by the vermin as to very nearly resemble a case of scabbing from small-pox, being covered with sores from head to foot, so as scarcely to be able to touch a well portion of the skin with the point of the finger.

Their appearance was such in the way of filth and dirt, as to convince any one that they had not had an opportunity for ablution for weeks and months. Several were in a state of semi-insanity, and all seemed, and acted, and talked, like children, in their desires for food, &c. Very few of them had blankets or clothing, some in a state of semi-nudity.

Upon being questioned upon the causes of their condition, the testimony was universal:— starvation, exposure, and neglect, while prisoners at Richmond and Belle Isle.

Their universal declaration was, in reference to their living. that they were provided with only one small portion of corn-bread per day, which was made simply from cornmeal and water, without salt, not larger than a man's hand; it was about an inch and a quarter thick. This was the portion for the day. They sometimes got small portions of meat once a day, two days in a week. Several of them told me that they had been able to get occasionally a small piece of the flesh of a dog, which they had cooked and eaten with great relish, and that they had caught rats and eaten them in the same way. Many of them believed that the meat issued to them was cut from the bodies of mules.

They said, while on Belle Isle they had no means of shelter, but were obliged to huddle together in heaps, to protect themselves from the inclement weather;— often one or two blankets in thickness covering five or six persons;— often lying one upon another in tiers, and changing places as they became tired out. They state that they had little or no shelter while prisoners at Belle Isle.

We were obliged to treat them as children, in regulating their diet in the hospital, having to restrain their over-eating, and confine them to a concentrated but nourishing and generous diet.

Several cases had no disease whatever, but suffered from extreme emaciation and starvation. The limb of one of these men could be spanned with the thumb and finger, just above the knee. This patient, a boy of nineteen years old, would not weigh over fifty pounds then, though in health probably one hundred and thirty-five pounds. This was not a solitary instance, many others being extremely emaciated. Many presenting the appearance of mere living skeletons, with the skin drawn tightly over the bones.

Many of them were laboring under such diseases as dropsy, pulmonary consumption, scurvy, mortification from cold, several having lost one-half of both feet from this cause.

Several were afflicted with very severe bed-sores, caused by lying in the sand without shelter. One man, unable to lie in any other way but on his face, and lived about four weeks in this way.

Up to the present time. of the number received, (one hundred and five), forty-two have died. All gave evidence of extensive visceral disease, of which starvation. cold, and neglect, were undoubtedly the primary cause. Some of the cases sank from extreme debility, without any evidence of disease as the cause of death.

A. CHAPEL,
Surgeon U. S. A.

Affirmed to and subscribed
before me, June 2d, 1864.
D. P. BROWN, JR.,
United States Commissioner.

Testimony of Miss D. L. Dix, taken at Baltimore, Maryland, June 1st, 1864.

Miss D. L. DIX *sworn and examined:*—

Last winter I was at Annapolis and examined many hundred returned prisoners. I inquired of these men exactly the manner in which they were fed and treated on Belle

Island, examined them individually, and by sixes and sevens. I saw no disposition on the part of these men to exaggerate their sufferings.

Inquiring from what causes they had suffered most severely, whether rapid marches, exposure to inclement weather, lack of apparel, or hunger,— the answer was invariably, "From hunger while at Belle Island." I inquired the amount of animal food allowed a day, when they had any at all; they replied that an iron-bound bucket, filled with packed meat, was the allowance for one hundred men; the weight of bucket and meat would be twenty-five pounds. When cooked this afforded a very small quantity for each man.

As Winter and Spring advanced, the only food supplied was corn-meal mixed with water and roughly baked. This bucket of meat I speak of was allowed them about twice a week, with a very little rice in the autumn. I understand that in the hospitals they occasionally had a little boiled rice, to which was sometimes added a very small quantity of brown sugar or molasses.

I gather from Confederate authority as well as from our returned prisoners,— and a Confederate official whose evidence cannot be questioned in that matter, declared, that the sole sustenance at Belle Island was corn-meal and water,— that of the numbers remaining at Belle Island, then about eight thousand, about twenty-five died daily; that the mortality in Georgia was still greater, and that it would be but a few weeks before the deaths would count fifty a day.

Another fact which he affirmed as a reason for withholding so much from our prisoners, sent by their friends and the Government, was the cruel and severe restrictions imposed on their men in our hands.

I had visited those very prisoners to whom he referred at Point Lookout; they were supplied with vegetables, with the best wheat bread, and fresh or salt meat three times daily in abundant measure — the full Government ration.

In the camp of about nine thousand rebel prisoners, there were but four hundred reported to the surgeon; of these, one hundred were confined to their beds, thirty were very sick, and perhaps fifteen or twenty would never recover.

The hospital food consisted of beef tea, beef soup, rice, milk, milk punch, milk gruel, lemonade, stewed fruits, beef-steak, vegetables and mutton: white sugar was employed in cooking. The supplies were, in fact, more ample and abundant than in hospitals where our own men were under treatment.

To return to the condition of the Federal prisoners on Belle Island, there was at no time adequate shelter for the entire number till late in spring, when the number had been greatly reduced by transfer to Georgia, exchanges and death.

I was told that in the morning it was not uncommon to find men dead from exposure and rain.

I have repeatedly seen the exchanged prisoners reduced to the lowest extremity through want of food. Of more than four hundred landed in Baltimore, some little time since, nearly, if not the entire number, were suffering from the effects of hunger; more than one hundred of these were taken a few yards across the wharf, to the hospital, on stretchers; seven died before they could be taken into the building, and seven more that same night. Their clothing was filthy to the last degree; they were covered with vermin; they were the merest bundles of bones and skin, and some bones piercing the flesh. The cries of these poor men for food were pitiful in the extreme.

In addition to their other sufferings, many had lost portions of their feet by frost. The minds showed the weakness of the body. Some were reduced to idiocy. They would entreat for an apple or a bit of meat to look at, if they could not be allowed solid food. Many of these poor creatures died, and others, I understand from surgeons, are enfeebled for life.

Many of these prisoners when brought on the flag-of-truce boat, were observed to clasp their hands and fix their gaze upon the American flag: "It is enough, thank God, we are at home." A remarkable trial of disinterestedness: Rev. M. Hall said, "What can I do for you, my boys?" "Hasten exchanges and bring away our comrades."

A gentleman of Washington, who had been permitted to convey a body for burial to the South, on board the flag-of-truce boat, remarked that all the rebel prisoners were in vigorous health, equipped in clothes furnished by the United States Government; many of them with blankets and haversacks, while we received in return not one able-bodied man at that time. I have witnessed this fact myself, on other occasions on the flag-of-truce boats.

The rations served to the prisoners on Belle Island, whether drawn from supplies furnished by the Federal Government, or through the individual liberality of Northern citizens, were never dispensed in sufficient quantities by the Confederate authorities to satisfy hunger.

I have seen tons of provisions shipped on the flag-of-truce boat from the North, for the relief of our prisoners at Richmond. Little or nothing came from the South for rebel prisoners at the North. Clothing and blankets were sent by our Government to the prisoners in quantities, but not fully distributed.

One reason why our men were so wholly destitute of clothing at a late season, was the temptation they were under to give them away for a biscuit, or a small quantity of food, to save them from starvation.

D. L. DIX.

Sworn to and subscribed before me,
June 1, 1864.
D. P. BROWN, JR.,
United States Commissioner.

I certify that the foregoing testimony was taken and reduced to writing in presence of the respective witnesses, and by them sworn or affirmed to in my presence, at the times, places, and in the manner set forth.

D. P. BROWN, JR.,
United States Commissioner.

Testimony of Joseph B. Abbott, Special Relief Agent United States Sanitary Commission, taken at Washington, D. C., June 3rd, 1864.

COMMISSIONERS PRESENT.—Mr. Wilkins, Dr. Wallace, Mr. Walden.

Joseph B. Abbott, aged twenty-eight years, Agent of Special Relief Department, United States Sanitary Commission. Holds his commission as Chief Assistant, Special Relief Department, United States Sanitary Commission. Is a native of New Hampshire, has been a resident of North Carolina, resided in North Carolina nearly four years, prior to the war. Has been engaged with the United States Sanitary Commission since March 12th, 1862.

During the past Spring, since February, my position has given me means of observation of returned prisoners from Richmond, Belle Island, Danville, Salisbury, and Columbia, but directly from Richmond. I first came in contact at Fortress Monroe with prisoners on flag-of-truce boats, from City Point to Annapolis. The men had no blankets, but what were said to have been furnished them at City Point by the United States Government. Very few had coats; many had no shirts; pants, poor, ragged and dirty; clothing all dirty; skin very filthy, and covered with vermin. One man had convulsions all the time during the trip. Assistant Surgeon Dr. Fry told me that they were caused by vermin. The man was much emaciated; vermin very thick upon his body — common body lice. He was scratching as at lice, and throwing them off him and slapping them with his blanket.

This is a general statement of all my observation.

My experience extended over three boat loads. No difference in the condition of the prisoners' clothing. The condition of the men on the last boat as to physical state, was worse than all previous. Two or three boat loads have arrived since my services ceased. Mr. Thompson, one of the United States Sanitary Commission Agents, accompanied the men on these boats. Mr. Thompson is now at White House, Virginia, on the Pamunky river. Cannot communicate with him by telegraph.

In general aspect and condition of returned prisoners, all were more or less emaciated. Of the first boat load, three-fifths very much so. Of second and third boats, four-fifths very much so. The condition of some of those who were less emaciated than others was owing to their having money with which they purchased provisions. I believe the fact from statements made by them on my inquiry. My attention was drawn to the fact by the Assistant Surgeon. I could pick out the men that had money by their physical condition.

Clothing was usually taken from them by their captors before their arrival at Richmond. Money was taken from them officially just before entering prison, except those that had succeeded in secreting it. I believe these facts from statements made by the men. They were also credited with the amounts, and were told that when released the amounts would be returned. I heard of no soldier who had it returned to him. In case of officers it was sometimes returned in Confederate currency.

On the first boat load there was about one hundred and fifty on cots sick,— with diarrhœa generally. Many of these one hundred and fifty men had the scurvy; great many suffering from pneumonia. Often heard the physician say that these disorders were due to confinement, exposure, and bad food. In all I saw some ten or twelve dying on the boats. From the last boat I saw five come off on shore in a dying state. I saw one man die on the boat; the Doctor said his death was caused by starvation. Saw one already dead on the boat at Fortress Monroe. The Doctor said his death was caused by eating. He died from eating too much after he had been starved. He obtained this over amount of food after having come into our hands.

The Doctor said that he had to be very cautious in giving them their rations, or they would injure themselves by getting too much; that several had died in consequence of eating too much, which they obtained from their comrades, who were too feeble and too far gone to eat the rations which were given them. Some would secrete their rations and try to get a second ration. The Assistant Surgeon told me that the one I had seen dead had eaten three rations which he had obtained from his comrades.

The prisoners on board the boats stated that their diseases and sufferings, such as I witnessed, were caused by want of protection from wet and cold, and by insufficiency and bad food; this was their invariable statement.

The Union prisoners were not at all vindictive, and expressed a desire to have the rebel prisoners well clothed and fed; this was the case with all the men I spoke to on the subject on the three boats.

My reason for making this inquiry was the remark of the Union prisoners in regard to the healthy condition of the rebel prisoners who were exchanged. Some of them remarked that it would make the condition of the Union prisoners worse if they attempted to retaliate, and would do no good. The general idea as expressed by the men was, that they did not wish to see the rebel prisoners treated as they had been.

I have been on the battle-field and in hospitals and witnessed much suffering, but never did I experience so sad and deplorable a condition of human beings, as that of the paroled Union prisoners just from Belle Island, and the rebel prisons of the South, emaciated by starvation, with impaired minds, vision, powers of speech and hearing, occasioned by want of sufficiency of wholesome food, exposure to the cold and inclement storms of wind and rain. I believe from what I have seen and experienced among our unfortunate prisoners on board the flag-of-truce boats, that their barbarous treatment and sufferings which they endured while confined in the military prisons of the South can hardly be exaggerated.   J. B. ABBOTT.

Sworn and subscribed before me at Washington, D. C., this 3d day of June, A. D. 1864.
M. H. N. KENDIG,
Notary Public.

QUARTERLY REPORT

Of the Hospitals for the Federal prisoners, Richmond, Va., furnished by Surgeon-General, C. S. A., April 1, 1864. Obtained by a paroled and returned Federal prisoner.

DISEASES.	Jan. Cases	Jan. Deaths	Feb. Cases	Feb. Deaths	Mar. Cases	Mar. Deaths	DISEASES.	Jan. Cases	Jan. Deaths	Feb. Cases	Feb. Deaths	Mar. Cases	Mar. Deaths
Febris Cont. Communis	5		3	1	10	2	Anasarca	6	4	7	2	8	7
" Int. Quart.	6		23		20	5	Ascites	1		2	1		
" " Tertiana	4		20				Hydrothorax					1	
" Remittent	10		20		11	4	Rheumatism Acute	11		23		12	1
" Typhoides	18	12	35	28	35	20	" Chronica	40	4	42	12	14	3
Erysipelas	11	1	3	1	1	1	Abscessus	2		2			
Rubeola	14	1	15	7	6	4	Anthrax					1	
Variola } Convales-					77		Ulcus			4		1	
Varioloides } cents							Contusio					1	1
Diarrhœa Acuta	31	18	100	13	27	13	Gelatio					15	0
" Chronica	229	193	317	265	283	230	Vulnus Incisum			1			
Dysentery Acuta	36	4	23	6	9	3	Lumbago	1					
" Chronica	18	12	34	24	27	20	Vulnus Sclopiticum	20	1	27		20	3
Dyspepsia	4	3	1		2	1	Otitis	1					
Enteritis			1				Debilitas	15	4	107	17	37	21
Gastritis							Hæmorrhois			2	1	6	2
Hepatitis Chronica	4		2	1	4	3	Morbi Cutis			6		9	
Icterus	4		1		4	3	Scorbutus	7		7	3	17	7
Parotitis			3		3		Tumores			1			
Tonsillitis			7	3			Dry Gangrene from frozen Feet	27	3	23	4		
Asthma	1	1	1	1									
Bronchitis Acuta	21		46	7	12	3		646	311	1252	524	881	561
" Chronica	20	6	45	16	50	39							
Catarrhus Epidemicus			1										
" "	10	1	35	4	17	9	Total						2779
Laryngitis			2		1	1	Total Deaths						1396
Phthisis Pulmonalis	6	2	8	5	1	1							
Pleuritis	9	1	10	5	12	9							
Pneumonia	63	38	207	97	120	109							
Anæmia			1										
Cerebritis			1										
Epilepsia	1		1										
Meningitis	1	1	1										
Neuralgia	1		3		1								
Paralysis	1				1	1							
Tetanus	4	2											
Bubo Syphiliticum	1												
Cystitis			1										
Gonorrhœa	5		1		1								
Nephritis	1		4		6								
Orchitis	1		1										
Syphilitis Primitiva	2				1								
" Consect	2		2										

A true copy.
(Signed) A. R. ROOT,
Colonel Commanding, Camp Parole.

A true copy.
B. A. VANDERKIEFT,
Surgeon U. S. Vols. in charge U. S. General Hospital, Division No. 1, Annapolis, Md.

The Commission have received a letter from Col. A. R. Root, Commanding, &c., stating that he has satisfactory evidence of the authenticity and reliableness of this "Quarterly Report."

EVIDENCE RELATING TO UNITED STATES STATIONS FOR REBEL PRISONERS.

Letter from Quartermaster-General, M. C. Meigs, United States Army.

QUARTERMASTER-GENERAL'S OFFICE,
WASHINGTON, D. C., July 6th, 1864.

Dr. ELLESLIE WALLACE, Philadelphia.

SIR,— I have the honor to acknowledge the receipt of your letter of the 20th ult., in which, in behalf of a Committee of the United States Sanitary Commission, you make inquiry in relation to the condition and treatment of rebel prisoners of war in our hands.

In reply, you are respectfully informed that such prisoners are treated with all the consideration and kindness that might be expected of a humane and Christian people. The rations allowed to them are ample and of good quality. The reduction recently made in the prisoner's ration was for the purpose of bringing it nearer to what the rebel authorities profess to allow their soldiers, and no complaint has been heard of its insufficiency.

Suitable provision has been made by the Government for supplying the prisoners with all necessary clothing and blankets; and at each depot there is a sutler, authorized to sell to them, at reasonable rates, certain prescribed articles of comfort and convenience, such as our soldiers desire to purchase.

Fuel is provided by the army regulations, and is liberally furnished.

Shelter is not denied to any "during the inclement and cold season," and for those who require them, comfortable hospital accommodations, and skilful medical and surgical attention are provided.

The Commissary-General of Prisoners informs me that he has heard of no order to shoot prisoners for being at the windows or near them, and he does not believe that orders of that character have any where been given. He has heard of no prisoners being shot under such circumstances.

General Butler did, in the early part of this year, offer to exchange prisoners, grade for grade, and man for man, of those at Point Lookout, and two other places, but the proposition was not acceded to by the rebel authorities.

Your inquiries are thus substantially answered.

I enclose copies of the orders of the Commissary-General of Prisoners, regulating the conduct and treatment of prisoners of war, and the rations they now receive.*

I am, very respectfully,
Your obedient servant,
M. C. MEIGS,
Quartermaster-General.

* Printed in this Appendix.

Testimony taken at Fort Delaware, June 21st, 1864.

COMMISSIONERS PRESENT.— Dr. Wallace, Judge Hare.

Captain GILBERT S. CLARK, *sworn and examined:*—

I came to this post 18th March, 1862, and the Subsistence Department at this post has been under my charge since May, 1862.

The rations were as follow :
Bread — 18 ounces per ration ; or,
Corn Meal — 20 ounces per ration.
Beef — 1 pound per ration ; or,
Bacon or Pork — $\frac{3}{4}$ pound per ration.
Beans — 8 quarts per one hundred men; or,
Hominy or Rice — 10 pounds per one hundred men.
Sugar — 14 pounds per one hundred men.
Rio Coffee — 7 or 9 pounds per hundred men.
Adamantine Candles — 5 per one hundred men ; or,
Tallow Candles — 6 per one hundred men.
Soap — 4 pounds per one hundred men.
Salt — 2 quarts per one hundred men.
Molasses — 4 quarts per one hundred men, twice per week.
Potatoes — 1 pound per man, three times per week.

When beans were issued, hominy or rice not issued.

These were the rations to which the prisoners were entitled. Bread was issued, in point of fact, and not corn meal. Fresh beef was issued, during this time, four times a week. When we had to give them hard bread they received a pound. When fresh beef was given, a pound and a quarter was given, and a less proportion of salt meat.

This was done by orders of the commanding officer, with a view to the sanitary condition of the men.

According to instructions for the Commissary-General of Prisoners, a fund was created by selling all surplus rations, under regulations, and with this fund were purchased vegetables in addition to the regular rations. The order referred to, under which this course was adopted, was as follows :

CIRCULAR.

* * * * *

" V. A general fund, for the benefit of the prisoner, will be made by withholding from their rations all that can be spared without inconvenience to them, and selling this surplus, under existing regulations, to the Commissary, who will hold the funds in his hands, and be accountable for them, subject to the commanding officer's order to cover purchases. The purchases with the fund will be made by or through the Quartermaster, with the approval or order of the commanding officer, the bills being paid by the Commissary, who will keep an account book, in which will be carefully entered all receipts and payments, with the vouchers; and he will keep the commanding officer advised, from time to time, of the amount of this fund. At the end of the month he will furnish the commanding officer with an account of the fund for the month, showing the receipts and disbursements, which account will be forwarded to the Commissary-General of Prisoners, with the remarks of the commanding officer. With this fund will be purchased all such articles as may be necessary for the health and comfort of the prisoners, and which would otherwise have to be purchased by the Government; among these articles are all table furniture and cooking utensils, articles for policing purposes, bedticks and straw, the means of improving or enlarging the barracks accommodation, extra pay to clerks who have charge of the camp, post-office, and who keep the accounts of moneys deposited with the commanding officer, &c., &c."

The provisions, according to my return, actually issued, were the same as for the garrison troops. The rations detailed above were the rations actually given to the men. The amount drawn on the books, for their account, was larger — and as large as that issued to the garrison, with the exception of flour or bread, which was eighteen ounces instead of twenty-two ounces. When I say actually issued, I mean when entered on my returns as issued. The difference between the amount thus issued, and the amount given as above, was sold and converted into a fund for the benefit of the prisoners, as I have stated, according to the order of which I have given an extract.

This fund was expended and applied for their use in the purchase of extra vegetables and articles of comfort.

This course is pursued towards our own troops in camp and garrison; the surplus which they do not use being sold for their benefit to the Commissary of Subsistence, and regularly entered, and the proceeds applied to their use.

The surplus rations sold for the prisoners were about the same as those sold for the garrison at the same time, showing that the amount actually consumed by the prisoners was about the same, per man, as that consumed by the garrison. When hard bread is issued, prisoners not unfrequently leave a portion of it on the table. A large amount of bread has been found stowed away by them in the barracks. The rations are precisely the same as that used for garrison, and of very good quality.

My expenditures for vegetables alone, for the use of the prisoners, out of the fund arising from the sale of the surplus rations, amounted, at times, as high as from $2,000 to $3,000 a month. For instance, I would buy extra quantities of potatoes and onions, turnips, cabbage, pickles, carrots.

I have frequently asked my overseers if the prisoners complained of not having enough, and if they did, to give them more, and to let no man want, as I could afford to do from the savings. During all the time I have been here, I have scarcely heard a complaint. No material change was made in the rations given to the prisoners till the first of this month. (June '64); since this date, the following has been the ration given the prisoners:

The rations *issued* on the returns remained the same as before. The amount *given* was reduced to the following quantity, by order of the Secretary of War:

"B."

"RATION:

"Pork or Bacon,	10 ozs.	(in lieu of fresh beef.)
Fresh Beef,	14 "	
Flour, or Soft Bread,	16 "	
Hard Bread,	14 "	(in lieu of Flour or Soft Bread.)
Corn Meal,	16 "	(in lieu of Flour or Bread.)
Beans or Peas,	12½ lbs.	
or, Rice, or Hominy,	8 "	
Soap,	4 "	to 100 rations.
Vinegar,	3 qts	
Salt,	3¾ lbs.	
Potatoes,	15 "	

Sugar and coffee, or tea, will be issued only to the sick and wounded, on the recommendation of the surgeon in charge, at the rate of twelve (12) pounds of sugar, five (5) pounds of ground or seven (7) pounds of green coffee, or one (1) pound of tea, to the one hundred rations. This part of the ration will be allowed only for every other day."

The difference between the ration given and the ration issued continues to be sold, and the proceeds applied to the benefit of the prisoners, as before. The consequence is that the surplus fund for their use is larger.

I refer to the circulars issued by the War Department, April 20th, 1864, and June 1st, 1864, as containing the regulations under which I am now acting, hereto appended, marked "A" and "B."

The bread, as now issued, is made one-fifth of corn meal and four-fifths of flour. This change was made at the request of the prisoners. I use the same quality of bread.

GILBERT S. CLARK,
Captain and C. S. Vol.

Sworn to and subscribed before me,
June 21st, 1864.

D. P. BROWN, JR.,
United States Commissioner.

"A."

"OFFICE OF COMMISSARY-GENERAL OF PRISONERS, WASHINGTON, *April* 20, 1864.

"[CIRCULAR.]

"By authority of the War Department, the following Regulations will be observed at all stations where prisoners of war and political or State prisoners are held. The regulations will supersede those issued from this office July 7, 1861:

I. The Commanding Officer at each station is held accountable for the discipline and good order of his command, and for the security of the prisoners, and will take such measures, with the means placed at his disposal, as will best secure these results. He will divide the prisoners into companies, and will cause written reports to be made to him of their condition every morning, showing the changes made during the preceding twenty-four hours, giving the names of the "joined," "transferred," "deaths," &c. At the end of every month Commanders will send to the Commissary-General of Prisoners a Return of Prisoners, giving names and details to explain "alterations." If rolls of "joined" or "transferred" have been forwarded during the month, it will be sufficient to refer to them on the return according to forms furnished.

II. On the arrival of any prisoners at any station, a careful comparison of them with the rolls which accompany them will be made, and all errors on the rolls will be corrected. When no roll accompanies the prisoners, one will immediately be made out, containing all the information required, as correct as can be, from the statements of prisoners themselves. When the prisoners are citizens, the town, county and State from which they come will be given on the rolls under the headings — Rank, Regiment, and Company. At stations where prisoners are received frequently, and in small parties, a list will be furnished every fifth day — the last one in the month may be for six days — of all prisoners received during the preceding five days. Immediately on their arrival, prisoners will be required to give up all arms and weapons of every description, of which the Commanding Officer will require an accurate list to be made. When prisoners are forwarded for exchange, duplicate parole rolls, signed by the prisoners, will be sent with them, and an ordinary roll will be sent to the Commissary-General of Prisoners. When they are transferred from one station to another, an ordinary roll will be sent with them, and a copy of it to the Commissary-General of Prisoners. In all cases, the officer charged with conducting prisoners will report to the officer under whose orders he acts, the execution of his service, furnishing a receipt for the prisoners delivered, and accounting by name for those not delivered; which report will be forwarded, without delay, to the Commissary-General of Prisoners.

III. The hospital will be under the immediate charge of the senior Medical Officer present, who will be held responsible to the Commanding Officer for its good order and the proper treatment of the sick. A fund for this hospital will be created as for other hospitals. It will be kept separate from the fund of the hospital for the troops, and will be expended for the objects specified, and in the manner prescribed in paragraph 1212, Revised Regulations for the Army of 1863, except that the requisition of the Medical Officer in charge, and the bill of purchase, before payment, shall be approved by the Commanding Officer. When this "fund" is sufficiently large, it may be expended also for shirts and drawers for the sick, the expense of washing clothes, articles for policing purposes, and all articles and objects indispensably necessary to promote the sanitary condition of the hospital.

IV. Surgeons in charge of hospitals where there are prisoners of war will make to the Commissary-General of Prisoners, through the Commanding Officer, semi-monthly reports of deaths, giving names, rank, regiment, and company; date and place of capture; date and cause of death; place of interment, and No. of grave. Effects of deceased prisoners will be taken possession of by the Commanding Officer, the money and valuables to be reported to this office (see note on blank reports), the clothing of any value to be given to such prisoners as require it. Money left by deceased prisoners, or accruing from the sale of their effects, will be placed in the Prison Fund.

V. A fund to be called "The Prison Fund," and to be applied in procuring such articles as may be necessary for the health and convenience of the prisoners, not expressly provided for by General Army Regulations, 1863, will be made by withholding from their rations such parts thereof as can be conveniently dispensed with. The Abstract of Issues to Prisoners, and Statement of the Prison Fund, shall be made out. commencing with the month of May, 1864, in the same manner as is prescribed for the Abstract of Issues to Hospital and Statement of the Hospital Fund, (see paragraphs 1209, 1215, and 1246, and Form 5, Subsistence Department, Army Regulations, 1863), with such modifications in language as may be necessary. The ration for issue to prisoners will be composed as follows, viz.:

Hard Bread,	14 oz. per one ration, or 18 oz. Soft Bread, one ration.
Corn Meal,	18 oz. per one ration.
Beef,	14 " " "
Bacon or Pork,	10 " " "
Beans,	6 qts. per 100 men.
Hominy or Rice,	8 lbs. " "
Sugar,	14 " " "
R. Coffee, or	5 lbs. ground, or 7 lbs. raw, per 100 men.
Tea,	18 oz. per 100 men.
Soap,	4 " " "
Adamantine Candles,	5 candles per 100 men.
Tallow Candles,	6 " " "
Salt,	2 qts. " "
Molasses,	1 qt. " "
Potatoes,	30 lbs. " "

When beans are issued, hominy or rice will not be. If at any time it should seem advisable to make any change in this scale, the circumstances will be reported to the Commissary-General of Prisoners for his consideration.

VI. Disbursements to be charged against the Prison Fund will be made by the Commissary of Subsistence, on the order of the Commanding Officer; and all such expenditures of funds will be accounted for by the Commissary, in the manner prescribed for the disbursements of the Hospital Fund. When in any month the items of expenditures on account of the Prison Fund cannot be conveniently entered on the Abstract of Issues to Prisoners, a list of the articles and quantities purchased, prices paid, statement of services rendered, &c., certified by the Commissary as correct, and approved by the Commanding Officer, will accompany the Abstract. In such cases it will only be necessary to enter on the Abstract of Issues the total amount of funds thus expended.

VII. At the end of each calendar month, the Commanding Officer will transmit to the Commissary-General of Prisoners a copy of the "Statement of the Prison Fund," as shown in the Abstract of Issues for that month, with a copy of the list of expenditures specified in preceding paragraph, accompanied by vouchers, and will endorse thereon, or convey in letter of transmittal, such remarks as the matter may seem to require.

VIII. The Prison Fund is a credit with the Subsistence Department, and at the request of the Commissary-General of Prisoners, may be transferred by the Commissary-General of Subsistence in manner prescribed by existing Regulations for the transfer of Hospital Fund.

IX. With the Prison Fund may be purchased such articles not provided for by regulations as may be necessary for the health and proper condition of the prisoners, such as table furniture, cooking utensils, articles for policing, straw, the means for improving or enlarging the barracks or hospitals, &c. It will also be used to pay clerks, and other employees engaged in labors connected with prisoners. No barracks or other structures will be erected or enlarged, and no alterations made, without first submitting a plan and estimate of the cost to the Commissary-General of Prisoners, to be laid before the Secretary of War for his approval; and in no case will the services of clerks or of other employees be paid for without the sanction of the Commissary-General of Prisoners. Soldiers employed with such sanction will be allowed 40 cents per day when employed as clerks, stewards, or mechanics; 25 cents a day when employed as laborers.

X. It is made the duty of the Quartermaster, or, when there is none, the Commissary, under the orders of the Commanding Officer, to procure all articles required for the prisoners, and to hire clerks or other employees. All bills for service, or for articles purchased, will be certified by the Quartermaster, and will be paid by the Commissary on the order of the Commanding Officer, who is held responsible that all expenditures are for authorized purposes.

XI. The Quartermaster will be held accountable for all property purchased with the Prison Fund, and he will make a return of it to the Commissary-General of Prisoners at the end of each calendar month, which will show the articles on hand on the first day of the month; the articles purchased, issued and expended during the month; and the articles remaining on hand. The return will be supported by abstracts of the articles purchased, issued, and expended, certified by the Quartermaster, and approved by the Commanding Officer.

XII. The Commanding Officer will cause requisitions to be made by his Quartermaster for such clothing as may be absolutely necessary for the prisoners, which requisition will be approved by him, after a careful inquiry as to the necessity, and submitted for the approval of the Commissary-General of Prisoners. The clothing will be issued by the Quartermaster to the prisoners, with the assistance and under the supervision of an officer detailed for the purpose, whose certificate that the issue has been made in his presence will be the Quartermaster's voucher for the clothing issued. From the 30th of April to the 1st of October, neither drawers nor socks will be allowed, except to the sick. When army clothing is issued, buttons and trimmings will be taken off the coats, and the skirts will be cut so short that the prisoners who wear them will not be mistaken for United States soldiers.

XIII. The Sutler for the prisoners is entirely under the control of the Commanding Officer, who will require him to furnish the prescribed articles, and at reasonable rates. For this privilege the Sutler will be taxed a small amount by the Commanding Officer, according to the amount of his trade, which tax will be placed in the hands of the Commissary to make part of the Prison Fund.

XIV. All money in possession of prisoners, or received by them, will be taken charge of by the Commanding Officer, who will give receipts for it to those to whom it belongs. Sales will be made to prisoners by the Sutler on orders on the Commanding Officer, which orders will be kept as vouchers in the settlement of the individual accounts. The Commanding Officer will procure proper books in which to keep an account of all moneys deposited in his hands, these accounts to be always subject to inspection by the Commissary-General of Prisoners, or other inspecting officer. When prisoners are transferred from the post, the moneys belonging to them, with a statement of the amount due each, will be sent with them, to be turned over by the officer in charge to the officer to whom the prisoners are delivered, who will give receipts for the money. When prisoners are paroled, their money will be returned to them.

XV. All articles sent by friends to prisoners, if proper to be delivered, will be carefully distributed as the donors may request; such as are intended for the sick passing through the hands of the Surgeon, who will be responsible for their proper use. Contributions must be received by an officer, who will be held responsible that they are delivered to the person for whom they are intended. All uniform, clothing, boots, or equipments of any kind for military service, weapons of all kinds, and intoxicating liquors, including malt liquors, are among the contraband articles. The material for outer clothing should be gray, or some dark mixed color, and of inferior quality. Any excess of clothing, over what is required for immediate use, is contraband.

XVI. When prisoners are seriously ill, their nearest relatives, being loyal, may be permitted to make them short visits; but under no other circumstances will visitors be admitted without the authority of the Commissary-General of Prisoners. At those places where the guard is inside the enclosure, persons having official business to transact with the Commander or other officer will be admitted for such purposes, but will not be allowed to have any communication with the prisoners.

XVII. Prisoners will be permitted to write and to receive letters, not to exceed one page of common letter paper each, provided the matter is strictly of a private nature. Such letters must be examined by a reliable non-commissioned officer, appointed for that purpose by the Commanding Officer, before they are forwarded or delivered to the prisoners.

XVIII. Prisoners who have been reported to the Commissary-General of Prisoners will not be paroled or released except by authority of the Secretary of War.

W. HOFFMAN,
Col. 3d Infantry, Commissary-General of Prisoners.

OFFICIAL:
W. T. HART,
Assistant Adjutant General.

S. R. CRAIGE *sworn and examined:*—
I have been Quartermaster here since August, 1863. The amount of clothing issued to the prisoners from September 1st, 1863, to May 1st, 1864, by the Quartermaster's Department, will appear from the following statement prepared by me from the books:

QUARTERMASTER'S OFFICE, FORT DELAWARE,
June 21st, 1864.
CAPT. S. R. CRAIGE,
A. Q. M. Volunteers.

Statement of Clothing issued to Prisoners of War, from Sept. 1st, 1863, to May 1st, 1864:

7175 Pairs Drawers (Canton flannel).
6260 Shirts (Flannel).
8807 Pairs Woolen Stockings.
1094 Jackets and Coats.
3840 Pairs Bootees.
1310 Pairs Trowsers.
4378 Woolen Blankets.
2680 Great Coats.

The principal part of the clothing was issued in October and November, 1863, and every prisoner not having an overcoat and blanket of his own was provided with one.

All that were in want of clothing received it.

The barracks were kept comfortable by stoves; no stint in fuel that I know of; the attendants kept the fires up. Three hundred tons of coal provided by me, were consumed by the prisoners in the winter and spring. This, in addition to wood used for baking, and to the coal supplied by Capt. Clark. I am satisfied the prisoners were as comfortable as could be.

S. R. CRAIGE,
Captain and A. Q. M.

Sworn to and subscribed before me,
June 21st, 1864.

D. P. BROWN, JR.,
United States Commissioner.

Captain G. S. CLARKE, *recalled:*—

I have purchased and used for the prisoners about one thousand tons of coal during the winter. I would say, in my judgment, that the barracks were sufficiently warm during the season requiring fires. I was Quartermaster here, as well as Commissary, until Captain Craige assumed the Quartermaster's Department.

The destitute prisoners were supplied with sufficient clothing during the time I acted as Quartermaster.

GILBERT S. CLARK.

Attest:
D. P. BROWN, JR.,
United States Commissioner.

Captain GEORGE W. AHL, *sworn and examined:*—

My rank is Captain; Acting Assistant Adjutant-General for six months, and Commissary of Prisoners for about a year and a half.

Q. Can you state whether the rations issued to prisoners at this post were actually given them in full?

A. To the best of my knowledge and belief they were.

Q. Were the rations issued sufficient for their subsistence? had they at any time saved any rations, and was there any waste of their rations at any time?

A. The rations issued to them were at all times sufficient for their subsistence; and sometimes greatly in excess of what they could eat. In policing their barracks sometime ago we tore up the lower bunk boards, under which we found about eight (8) barrels of hard bread and meat, which they had secreted there, because there was more than they could eat. At that time we had only about three thousand prisoners here.

According to official monthly reports made to the Commissary-General of prisoners, there were at this post in July, 1863, 8,982 prisoners, of whom 111 died during the month.

August, 1863, 8,822 prisoners, of whom 169 died.
September, 1863, 6,490 " " 327 "
October, 1863, 2,987 " " 377 "
November, 1863, 2,822 " " 156 "
December, 1863, 2,765 " " 82 "
January, 1864, 2,600 " " 78 "
February, 1864, 2,655 " " 42 "
March, 1864, 5,712 " " 62 "
April, 1864, 6,149 " " 74 "
May, 1864, 8,126 " " 62 "
To June 21, 1864, 8,536 " " 42 "

The greater mortality during the summer and fall months of 1863, was attributable to the following causes: Small-pox; the majority of the prisoners not having been vaccinated before they came here, and those who were vaccinated had been vaccinated with impure matter: at all events, the vaccination resulted in breaking out over their body in sores; and from the prostrated condition of the prisoners from Vicksburg, a great many of whom had to be carried on their arrival here, from the boat to the hospital, and many of whom represented that they had been limited to half and quarter rations of an inferior quality during the siege of Vicksburg. Many died also from wounds received in different engagements. Many, when brought here, were suffering from chronic diarrhœa and other diseases. The general effect of our treatment of the prisoners at this post has resulted in great benefit to their physical condition. In reference to vaccination, being desirous of obtaining the true cause of its bad effects on their system, I inquired of them (the prisoners) the cause of it; they stated that they had been vaccinated by their own men with impure matter.

GEORGE W. AHL,
Captain and A. A. A. G. and
Commissary of Prisoners.

Sworn to and subscribed before me,
June 21st, 1864.

D. P. BROWN, JR.,
U. S. Commissioner.

Lieutenant A. G. WOLF, *sworn and examined:*—

I am a Lieutenant in charge of prisoners at Fort Delaware; have been here since 23d September, 1862; have had charge of the prisoners about eight months.

The order is that the men shall be sent out every day for air. The barracks are then entirely cleansed out. At one time we turned the prisoners out, and found enough of crackers to have paved the barracks two crackers deep, and they are an average of five hundred feet. They had stowed and concealed them away in various places. As a general thing, when the barracks were cleaned out, there were always a number of rations, bread and meat, found stowed away. We have always found a quantity of blankets and clothing stowed away under the floor during the winter season. We have allowed men two blankets apiece, and when they were delicate, three blankets and an overcoat.

They are allowed to bathe in the river twice a week. We have to take a guard to get some of them to go out to bathe. We issue a regular prisoner's ration of soap; we have found as much as ten pounds secreted in their haversacks.

They had five stoves within five hundred feet during winter, and were warm enough in their barracks.

There has never been an order to fire at any man looking out the windows, and no man has ever been fired at for looking out; there have been five men shot; three killed and two wounded here, since this has been a prison. One killed while in the river making his escape, about one hundred yards from the shore, at night; one killed for attempting to climb over the fence towards the river; one man was wounded—he died since—for committing a nuisance on the bank contrary to rule, and was ordered by the sentry to stop. He called the sentry "a Yankee son of a bitch," and would not stop. The ball wounded two men. The other one said that he deserved all he got. Another was killed accidentally, by the sentry shooting at one who was committing a nuisance, and who would not obey the order. These orders are to prevent nuisances occurring in the barracks, which would be destructive of health and cleanliness. Even with these rules, nuisances are not unfrequently committed.

Special orders No. 157 are the same as those I refer to, and are as follow:

SPECIAL ORDER No. 157.

HEADQUARTERS, FORT DELAWARE,
June 1, 1864.

The officer of the Guard must read and explain these orders to each *relief* of his Guard regularly before having it posted.

I. No sentinel must communicate with nor allow any person to communicate with any of the prisoners, nor permit any of the prisoners to go outside of the limits of their barracks, without the permission of the Commanding General or the officers in charge of the prisoners.

II. It is the duty of the sentinel to prevent the prisoners from *escaping*, or *cutting, defacing, or in any way damaging any of the Government property*, or from *committing any "Nuisance"* in or about their barracks, or from *using any abusive or insolent* LANGUAGE towards them, and from any violation of good order.

Should the sentinel detect any prisoner in violating these instructions, he must order him *three distinct times to halt!* and if the prisoner obeys the order, the sentinel must call for the Corporal of the Guard, and have the prisoner placed in arrest — but *should the prisoner fail to halt, when so ordered, the sentinel must enforce his order by bayonet or ball.*

III. The sentinels are required to exercise the utmost vigilance, and to exact from prisoners a strict compliance with these instructions, and must always be duly impressed with the nature and extent of their responsibility.

By command of BRIG. GEN'L SCHOEPF.
(Signed) GEO. W. AHL,
Captain and A. A. A. G.

They exist in all prisons.
A. G. WOLF.
Lieutenant and Commissary of Prisoners.

Sworn to and subscribed before me,
June 21st, 1864.
D. P. BROWN, JR.,
United States Commissioner.

Surgeon H. R. SILLIMAN, *sworn and examined:*—

I have been in charge here as Surgeon-in-Charge of the books since July, 1863. The condition of the prisoners, upon arriving here, was that generally of men suffering from over-exertion and bad diet; chronic diarrhœa and scurvy prevalent among them; they improved very materially shortly after their arrival here.

The sanitary conditions here were such as to be conducive to their health. Prisoners who arrived here from Vicksburg and the Mississippi Valley were laboring under miasmatic influences, under which a great number of them died. From their condition, I should judge they had been on a diet of salt meat. Some of the men arrived here in a good condition of health. The men from Gettysburg were generally in good health, though they soon broke down, showing the effect of their violent exertions; they rallied again under good food and good clothing. The condition of the men brought here within the last few months, captured in Virginia, has been better than that of those brought here heretofore. A large number of the men had never been vaccinated, and many others imperfectly so. The scars were imperfect, in my judgment. They vaccinated themselves in the barracks with pen-knives, after their arrival here, producing diseases of the blood and skin. In my experience, the proportion of the unvaccinated men, among the prisoners, is far greater than in our own army, for I have never known of an unvaccinated man in our army.

I consider the amount of food and clothing allowed to prisoners here, during the past winter, reasonably sufficient for the preservation of life and health.

I don't know of any man who has suffered from a want of food or clothing, and unable to procure them, on proper representations.

I do know of one man who was brought into the hospital last winter, during a severe spell, severely frost-bitten. I don't know how this occurred. This is the only instance that has come to my knowledge.

The men sent away from here were sometimes sick and sometimes well; they were in general well; and the physical condition of the well men was good. The sick were sent away under special orders, going as sick.

The order was from Surgeon-General Hammond; it was not an order to send away any who could not bear the journey: it was left to my discretion who to send away, and I sent none who I believed would die on the passage; I was careful about that.

I think the treatment of the sick prisoners here is equal to the treatment of our own sick men anywhere.

I expend as much as $1,700 per month, saved from the surplus rations, on delicacies for the sick.

H. R. SILLIMAN,
Assistant Surgeon U. S. A.

Sworn to and subscribed before me,
June 21st, 1864.
D. P. BROWN, JR.,
United States Commissioner.

Lieutenant A. G. WOLF, *recalled:*—

I am acquainted with the case of frost-bite spoken of by Dr. Silliman. The prisoners reported to me that the man was taken with cramps in the barracks; they exposed his person and rubbed him to ease the pain, and found that they could do no good, and then brought him to the hospital in that condition of exposure. I attributed the frost-bite to these circumstances.

A. G. WOLF,
Lieutenant and Commanding Prison

Attest,
D. P. BROWN, JR.,
United States Commissioner.

Surgeon Colin ARROTT, *sworn and examined:*—

I am acting assistant-surgeon at this place; have been here over two years. When I first came here the water used for drinking was rain water; and after I came here the water was brought from the Brandywine, in casks by sloops. I cautioned all the prisoners that came here against drinking the water of the Island, as it was unhealthy. They would frequently persist in doing it, although there was fresh water provided for them. They did this to save themselves from the trouble of going about a hundred yards for fresh water. They would dig little wells for the water, a few inches deep; I think that water produced sickness, though I frequently cautioned them, and at different times. This was two years ago.

For a year the water has been brought here in large quantities by boats. There are 30,000 gallons of water brought here now a day, besides what rain water is caught. There is now, and always has been, as far as I know, a full supply of water on the Island.

COLIN ARROTT,
Acting Assistant Surgeon.

Sworn to and subscribed before me,
June 21st, 1864.
D. P. BROWN, JR.,
United States Commissioner.

I certify that the foregoing testimony, taken at Fort Delaware, June 21st, 1864, was taken and reduced to writing by me, in the presence of the respective witnesses, and by them sworn to and subscribed in my presence, at the time and in the manner set forth.

D. P. BROWN, JR.,
U. S. Commissioner.

DAVID'S ISLAND, N. Y.

Testimony taken at De Camp General Hospital, U. S. A., David's Island, June 16th, 1864.

COMMISSIONER PRESENT.—Mr. Wilkins.

Deposition of Augustus Van Cortlandt, Acting Assistant Surgeon U. S. A.

I was on duty in this hospital when the last load of rebel prisoners arrived, during the latter part of July, 1863. Some were lodged in pavilions, and some in tents, which were in excellent order.

The prisoners had not been robbed or deprived of any of their private property, so far as my knowledge extends; on the contrary, the majority of patients under my charge possessed money, brought with them from the South to the hospital, and were never deprived of it.

They came in a filthy, horrible condition. Their dirty garments were removed and burned, and new hospital clothing furnished them at the expense of the United States Government, after they had been thoroughly cleansed and washed.

Their physical condition was bad in the extreme when they arrived; they were run down, and were the worst body of wounded men it has ever been my lot to see.

I had ten tents under my charge, which contained ninety-four rebel patients and nurses. The tents were twenty-eight by fifteen feet. The pavilions were one hundred and ninety-six feet in length, twenty-three feet in breadth, and twelve feet in height to the plate, and contained not more than eighty patients.

During the ensuing cold weather the prisoners were removed to the pavilions, and had all necessary fuel and warm clothing. I have never heard of any of the prisoners suffering from cold or exposure, so as to require medical treatment, nor of any having been frozen to death.

They were allowed, for exercise and recreation, the whole island inside of the line of sentries, having the same liberty, rations, diet and medical treatment, as the Federal sick and wounded have always had.

No rebel prisoners were ever fired upon, shot, or wounded, when on the Island, from any apprehension of their escaping, or from any other cause.

The supply of drinking water was of a good quality and abundant; and ice was supplied with liberal profusion, and sufficiency of water for washing, with plentiful allowances of soap, as well as combs, for their own private use.

The physical condition of the rebel prisoners, upon leaving the island, was very good, except a few cases of unhealed wounds.

AUG. VAN CORTLANDT, M. D.

Sworn to before me,
WARREN WEBSTER,
Assistant Surgeon U. S. A., in charge of Hospital.

Deposition of GEORGE W. EDWARDS, Acting Assistant Surgeon U. S. A.

I was stationed at this hospital when the rebel prisoners arrived, about the middle of July, 1863. They were placed in tents and pavilions, which had just been vacated by Union soldiers to make room for them. The dimension of the tents were twenty-eight feet by fifteen feet; the pavilions were one hundred and ninety-six feet in length, twenty-three feet in breadth, and twelve feet in height to the plate; not sealed over, and with numerous ventilators on the ridges. The tents were arranged to contain ten patients each, the pavilions to contain eighty; the number of patients never exceeded these numbers in either.

The prisoners had not been robbed by our men, as most of them had money, some had gold, greenbacks, and Confederate paper.

They were in rags, barefooted and bareheaded when they came, were frightfully filthy, and covered with vermin. Within three or four hours after their arrival, they had all been stripped of their rags, washed, and after being supplied with clean linen, placed in clean and well-aired beds.

Full suits of clothing, consisting of coats, pants, drawers, shirts, shoes and stockings, were subsequently issued to them by the United States Quartermaster. To distinguish them from our own soldiers, the buttons and six inches of the skirt of the coat were cut off.

Those who remained during the cold weather were abundantly supplied with fuel and warm clothing, and none required medical or surgical treatment in consequence of exposure to the cold; none were frozen to death.

They were allowed to go fishing or clamming, as they pleased, when they first came, till several escaped, when a line of sentinels was placed around the island upon the beach, inside of which they enjoyed all the privileges allowed to the Federal patients in the hospital.

None of the rebels were ever shot at, wounded or killed in any way while upon the island.

They receive medical and surgical treatment in all respects equal to that of Union soldiers. Nine-tenths of them were suffering from wounds. The mortality was not large, most of the deaths occurring from the severity of the wounds. They received the same rations and diet as our own patients.

The paper hereto attached, marked (A.)* formed the Diet Table during the time which the rebel prisoners were on the island. They had an abundance of good drinking water, with ice, an unlimited supply for bathing, plenty of soap, towels, combs, &c., &c., for their own comfort and cleanliness.

When the prisoners were removed, they were in excellent bodily condition, though many had not entirely recovered from their wounds; the majority of the prisoners left the island during the month of October, 1863. At one time there were about two thousand five hundred rebel prisoners upon the island.

I have been upon the medical staff of this hospital since its opening, in May, 1862, and it has been occupied by Union patients, both prior and subsequent to its occupation by rebel prisoners. G. W. EDWARDS.

Sworn to before me,
WARREN WEBSTER,
Assistant Surgeon U. S. A., in charge of Hospital.

DE CAMP GENERAL HOSPITAL,
DAVID'S ISLAND, NEW YORK,
June 17th, 1864.

We, the undersigned, Acting Assistant Surgeons U. S. A., employed in De Camp General Hospital, depose and say, that we

---

* The paper (A) here referred to, is the "DIET TABLE FOR GENERAL HOSPITALS, UNITED STATES ARMY."

have heard read the depositions of Augustus Van Cortlandt and George W. Edwards, Acting Assistant Surgeons U. S. A., of this date, and from our personal knowledge and actual experience confirm all that the said affidavits set forth as to the treatment of rebels, sick and wounded, during their confinement in this hospital.

We further depose that we have been members of the Medical Staff in this hospital, during and subsequent to its occupation by the rebel prisoners.

The Medical Staff numbered twenty-three Acting Assistant Surgeons, while the prisoners were on the island.

We would further depose that there were ample provisions of nurses; one nurse to every ten patients in the hospitals; and that the following provisions were made for the calls of nature: each pavilion was furnished with from two to four water-closets, and chairs and bed-pans were furnished for patients unable to reach the water-closet. The tents were furnished with bed-pans and chairs. Ample structures were made upon the beach for those able to walk.

JOHN HOWE, M. D., Acting Assistant Surgeon, U. S. A., further deposes and says, that on or about the first day of August 1863, while attending his duties in Pavilion 14, there was then and there present, the Rev. —— Brooks, Alabama Chaplain in the Confederate service, and prisoner of war, who addressed the rebel prisoners and said to them, "Well, boys, keep up your spirits, for you are getting a great deal better treatment here than you would get at home."

JOHN HOWE, M. D.,
Acting Assistant Surgeon, U. S. A.
WILLIAM BADGER,
GEORGE BADGER,
A. N. BROCKWAY,
WM. C. PRYER.

Sworn to before me,
WARREN WEBSTER,
Assistant Surgeon U. S. A., in charge of Hospital.

Deposition of the Rev. ROBERT LOWRY, Chaplin, U. S. A., Minister of Protestant Episcopal Church, Diocese of New York, under Bishop Potter.

Entered upon my duties here July 4, 1862, and have continued here until this time.

In my intercourse with the prisoners, I was guided systematically by the same rules with which I visited Union soldiers. The prisoners were equally well lodged with our own men. I remarked at the time of their arrival how neat and comfortable a provision had been made in the tents and pavilions for their comfort, with an ample supply of beds and bedding.

I met the first transport at Philadelphia, and returned on the same with them to David's Island. The prisoners were in a mos filthy condition, miserably clad, and covered with vermin. Each man received a bath and was immediately furnished with clean clothing, the old clothing being removed and burned. In the prosecution of my duties I was frequently present at their dinners, which were ample, superior, both as respects quantity and quality, to anything I have ever seen in hospital diet. The diet furnished to them was superior even to that of our own patients. This resulted from the fact that many little luxuries were furnished by private donation. There were other comforts and conveniences afforded them beyond those of food, clothing, and shelter.

A library of two thousand volumes, that had been previously used by our own soldiers, was at once thrown open to them, and every facility afforded for the use of the volumes. Being present as librarian, and taking each man's name as he received his book, the library was used by them far more than by our own people. As had been my practice, I went through the tents and pavilions with bibles and prayer books, making the special inquiry to every man, " Are you supplied?" And furnishing books in all cases where they were required.

Religious services were held in the chapel twice every Sunday, and two or three times during the week, at which they were invited to be present, and attended in such numbers that the chapel was always crowded, the capacity of the chapel being three hundred, and some occasions numbers stood at the windows during the entire service.

I was supervisor of the post office, and officially appointed to examine the contents of letters, which were mailed and forwarded on my approval. Paper and envelopes were furnished gratuitously, and post stamps, when needed, were supplied to the extent of one hundred and fifty dollars, to my knowledge, gratuitously. From three to five hundred letters were forwarded daily after the first arrival of prisoners.

The common expression in their letters as to their condition was that "we have everything we need, and could not be better off."

Funeral service was always performed over the dead, using the service of the Protestant Episcopal Church over the remains of the dead. A record was uniformly made of the names, company, and regiment, of the deceased, and date of death. This record was made independently of a formal Hospital register.
ROBERT LOWRY,
Chaplain U. S. A.

Sworn to before me,
WARREN WEBSTER,
Assistant Surgeon U. S. A., in charge.

THIRD SERIES. LIVING AGE. VOL. XXVII. 1264.

JOHNSON'S ISLAND, NEAR SANDUSKY, OHIO.

Testimony taken at Washington, D. C., June 3, 1864.

COMMISSIONERS PRESENT.—Mr. Wilkins, Dr. Wallace, Dr. Walden.

Surgeon CHAS. P. WILSON, *examined:*—

I was Acting Assistant Surgeon, United States Army. I was stationed at Johnson's Island, three miles from Sandusky, from the last week of October, 1863, to the last week of January, 1864. My duty was to attend to our men guarding the rebel prisoners, and also to attend at the Small-pox Hospital for rebel prisoners, and at the Post Hospital for our garrison; my position enabled me to see the general condition and the general treatment of the prisoners.

There could not be a more healthy or pleasant place than this island. Kelly's Island, a popular place of resort for pleasure and health, is about six miles from this island, and no better for these objects.

The buildings were good; in good order; they were new; say two years old; convenient and comfortable; they might have been better ventilated; the buildings were frame, and lined inside; they had rows of bunks, as in barracks, in three tiers—just the same as our men have in most of our barracks.

The rebel prisoners all had blankets, either their own or furnished by the United States Government, and were generally furnished with clothing by the United States Government—pants, shoes, hats, blouses, and underclothing and stockings,—until a short time before I left, then these were furnished to those only who actually needed them.

I have several times seen of an afternoon boxes carted in, and these articles distributed from the boxes among the prisoners, according to their wants.

I was there in extremely cold weather, when the supplies were teamed on the ice from the main land to Johnson's Island, a distance of three miles; the prisoners were provided against this severe weather by wood hauled every day for their use in stoves.

I consider that the wood was sufficient for comfortable supply, except for, say two or possibly three days, when the teams were engaged in bringing lumber and provisions for additional troops; during these two or three days the supply of wood was scant, and was the subject of complaint.

No prisoners were frost-bitten or came under medical treatment from cold and exposure, except some who attempted to escape. They all fared as well in this respect as our men do in barracks generally.

The sick men all had ticks filled with straw as beds; the hospital building for the rebels was lined and plastered.

There was abundant supply of good water from the lake by pipes and pumps; when the pipes froze they could go to the lake, under guard, and supply themselves, bringing it up in suitable vessels; they always had plenty of water to wash themselves and their clothes.

The rations of the prisoners were the same as those furnished to our own soldiers according to regulations.

The prisoners did not consume all their rations, for I know that there was a large prison fund formed from the savings.

During the hours of the day the prisoners were allowed to be in the open air as much as they pleased; there was abundant room for them all to take as much exercise as they required for health; they played games in the open air.

The surgeon in charge treated the sick rebels as he treated our sick; there was no difference at all, except when special articles of diet were sent to our men by their friends.

Some four hundred and sixty rebel privates were sent to some other prison in November; most of them had been on Johnson's Island for some months; when they left, taking them as a whole, their physical condition was excellent.

You could not have found the same number of prisoners anywhere in better condition.

C. P. WILSON,
Surgeon 128th Regiment O. N. G.

Sworn and subscribed before me, at Washington, D. C., this 3d day of June, 1864.

M. H. N. KENDIG,
Notary Public.

Depositions taken at Sandusky, Ohio.

MAJOR T. WOODBRIDGE, M. D., Surgeon in charge, *sworn and examined:* -

Q. What has been and is now your position in the army of the United States?

A. I am Surgeon of the 128th Regiment O. V. I., and Surgeon in charge of the Depot for Prisoners of War on Johnson's Island, near Sandusky, Ohio.

Q. How long have you held this position?

A. Since the establishment of the prison. I came to the island in February, 1862. The first prisoners came in April, 1862. I have had medical supervision of the prison from then until now.

Q. What is your opinion of Johnson's Island as to health and salubrity?

A. I believe Johnson's Island to be as favorable to health as the climate of Newport or Saratoga in summer, and as that of

Cincinnati or Dayton in winter. The latitude is about 41¼° North, longitude 82° 42' West. Height of lake above tide-water five hundred and sixty-five feet. The island rests upon a bed of Devonian limestone, which rises gradually from the shore to the centre, terminating in a ridge of limestone rock, thus affording complete natural drainage. The water used is principally that of the bay, which comes in fresh constantly from Lake Erie.

Q. What diseases, if any, are peculiar to Johnston's Island or the neighboring islands in Lake Erie?

A. I know of no diseases peculiar to those islands or prevalent in them. Johnson's Island is a small one, containing only about three hundred acres of land, and previous to the establishment of the prison, if I am correctly informed, was not inhabited by more than one family at a time; but the Peninsula, with Kelley's Island and the Put-in-Bay Islands, have been inhabited for between thirty and forty years. I have conversed frequently with some of the oldest citizens of the peninsula and the islands, but have never heard them speak of any liability to diseases, but such as is common to other parts of Ohio.

Q. Is there any truth in the assertion made by rebel authorities that residence on the island for a few months produces in a great number of prisoners dangerous and fatal pulmonary disorders?

A. Not the slightest.

Q. What has been the rate of mortality among the prisoners?

A. In 1862 — from April to December inclusive — the number of deaths was thirty-seven. During the year 1863 measles and smallpox were brought into the prison by prisoners sent from Alton and other prisons, and many wounded at the battles of Gettysburg, augmenting our mortality list above what it would otherwise have reached. The number of deaths for 1863 was ninety-seven. This makes, from the time of the first arrival of prisoners in April, 1862, to January 1st, 1864, (twenty-one months,) a mortality list of one hundred and thirty-four, out of an aggregate of six thousand four hundred and ten, received into the prison in that time. As there were exchanges and removals of prisoners, the number in prison never exceeded twenty-seven hundred at any one time.* Many of the prisoners came here with health impaired, by bad diet, exposure, and often by wounds received in battle. The bill of mortality owes little to the climate of the post, when we consider that men in prison, away from home and friends, are weighed down by anxieties and despondency, thus making the treatment of disease more difficult.

Q. Please state the number of prisoners now at the post?

A. About two thousand three hundred and six.*

Q. Please state the number of deaths during the past two months.

A. In the month of May there were five deaths; in the month of June only one.

Q. What accommodations are provided for the care of the sick?

A. The hospital building is one hundred and twenty-six by thirty feet, with a transverse hall six and a half feet wide in the centre. There are four wards, each forty-eight by thirty feet. There are eighty beds in all, giving to each patient, when the wards are full, seven hundred and twenty cubic feet of atmospheric air. The dispensary is furnished with all the medicines and stimulants furnished to hospitals for our own soldiers, and more than double the quantity is used by prisoners than by the same number of our troops. I have always had the assistance of competent Confederate surgeons, who cheerfully aid by giving their time to this duty. When there are no commissioned surgeons in prison, there are surgeons holding commissions in the line who do this duty. The cooking for the hospital is done by the most experienced and skilful cooks we can find in the prison.

In addition to rations, the sick are furnished with flour, potatoes, corn-meal, milk, butter, eggs, chickens, tea, &c., &c. The bedding is amply sufficient to make each patient comfortable. A pest-house is built outside the prison, to which all cases of smallpox, measles, or other contagions, are removed on first development.

J. WOODBRIDGE,
Surgeon 128th O. V. I.

Subscribed in my presence and sworn to before me at Sandusky, Ohio, this 5th day of July, 1864.

[SEAL.] HENRY C. BUSH,
Notary Public in and for Erie County, Ohio.

SURGEON EVERTMAN *examined:* —

Q. What position do you now hold at Depot Prisoners of War?

A. I act as chief medical officer of United States forces and military prison.

Q. How long have you held that position?

A. Since the 17th of May, 1864.

Q. What is your opinion of the general

---

* The average number of prisoners for the entire of the year 1863 was eleven hundred and fifteen.

* In May, 1864, there were two thousand one hundred and thirty-four, and in June, 1864, two thousand three hundred and nine.

healthfulness and salubrity of Johnson's Island?

A. The general condition of the troops and prisoners of war at this post has been unusually good and healthy. The hospital in the prison, during the past two months, scarcely ever had more than thirty inmates among an aggregate number of two thousand one hundred prisoners of war. The prevailing diseases, during this time, were diarrhœa, acute and chronic; a few cases of dysentery, and a small number of intermittent fever. I consider the island as healthy as any locality I have ever visited.

Q. Have you known any undue tendency to pulmonary disorders on this or the adjoining islands, or any part of the surrounding country?

A. I have not, at least not during the time that I have been stationed here. In the early part of the spring there were some few cases of pneumonia and bronchitis, but not any more so than would be expected even in a climate further south than this.

Q. What proportion of pulmonary complaints furnished in your hospital reports?

A. For the past six months the ratio has been as follows:

	Sick Treated.	Pulmonary Diseases.
January,	64	10
February,	66	5
March,	46	7
April,	91	1
May,	62	2
June,	80	5
Total,	409	30

Q. What is the appearance of the prisoners generally at this time?

A. Their appearance is very good. The prisoners confined at this depot are all rebel officers, but have very little pride to keep themselves or their quarters clean.

Q. Do the prisoners seem to gain or decline in health after their arrival here?

A. As a general thing their health improves. Most of the prisoners are robust and in good physical condition.

HENRY EVERTMAN,
Surgeon U. S. Vols., Chief Medical Officer.

Subscribed in my presence and sworn to before me at Sandusky, Ohio, this 5th day of July, 1864.

[SEAL.]   HENRY C. BUSH,
Notary Public in and for Erie County, Ohio.

Deposition taken at Kelley's Island.

GEORGE C. HUNTINGTON *examined:*

Q. How long have you resided on Kelley's Island?

A. Since the fall of 1838, with the exception of one year, from the fall of 1844 to the fall of 1845. Have been acquainted on the Island since 1835.

Q. What means have you of furnishing a statement of the character of the climate and sanitary condition of Kelley's Island, and the neighboring islands, and the surrounding country?

A. I have been in the habit, during the entire period of my residence on the island, of noting extremes of temperature, and such casual phenomena as would, in my opinion, have any bearing on the general health of the place; and for more than five years past have made three records daily of everything connected with the changes of the weather, in the manner prescribed by, and under the direction of, the Smithsonian Institution.

Q. Please state the latitude, longitude, and height above tide-water, of Kelley's Island; its population, and the general character of the island for salubrity.

A. My place of observation is in latitude 41° 35′ 44″ N., longitude 82° 42′ 32″ W. The level of Lake Erie is 565 feet above tide-water, and the island may in some places rise fifty or sixty feet above the level of the lake; but I think the mean height of the island would not vary much from twenty-five feet above the level of the lake. The population, in April last, was six hundred and fifty-one. As to the salubrity of the climate, the matter will be best determined by the statistics given in answer to the next question.

Q. What has been the percentage of mortality, annually, on your island?

A. In answer to this question I give an abstract from the records of the "Cemetery Association." This association was organized in May, 1853, since which time the whole number of interments has been 43
From this deduct, lost from vessels and washed ashore, ... 4
Died in Nashville, from wounds in battle, 1 — 5

Whole number of interments in 11 years, 38
To this add, died here and taken elsewhere for interment, ... 5

Whole number of deaths in 11 years, 43
From diseases reported as follows: —
Killed by premature blast 1, drowned 2,   3
Old age 3, intemperance 1, dropsy 1, .   5
Still-born and infants but a few days old, 8
Dysentery and summer complaint, . .   9
Inflammation of bowels, ...   3
Diseases affecting respiratory organs, .   5
Throat affection, age 76, age 50, . .   2
Fevers (one contracted in army hospital), 3
Childbirth 1, congestion of brain 1, . .   2
Fits 1, not specified 2, ...   3
                                   43

The average population of the island for this period of eleven years has been, as appears by the returns of the township assessor, 428, which would give an annual mortality of 3.9; but if we deduct casualties 3, still-born and infants, which, although born alive, had not vitality enough fairly to commence the journey of life, 8; and one from disease contracted in hospital in Nashville, 1, it will reduce the number of deaths properly chargeable to disease and old age to thirty-one, or an annual mortality of 2.82 in a population of 428. This would be an annual mortality from all causes of one per cent., and from disease, including old age, an annual mortality of less than seventy-three-hundredths of one per cent. (0.724.) By comparing these results with the tables of mortality in different sections of the country, the salubrity of our climate and the immunity from the ordinary diseases of the country enjoyed by the inhabitants of this island as compared with other localities, may be easily deduced.

Q. What is the distance of Kelley's from Johnson's Island, and is there any difference in the physical or sanitary peculiarities of the two islands?

A. Johnson's Island is about seven miles nearly due south from Kelley's Island, and I am not aware of any natural causes which should make any difference in the salubrity of climate or sanitary condition of the two localities, unless the difference in the water between Sandusky Bay and the open lake (the latter being considered rather more free from impurities) might be considered a difference, so far as it is used for culinary purposes or as a beverage.

Q. Is there any undue tendency to pulmonary disorders among the inhabitants of these islands?

A. By reference to the answer to a preceding question, it will be seen that the whole number of deaths from diseases affecting the respiratory organs in a period of eleven years, and in a population averaging four hundred and twenty-eight, was but five, and of this number one was a transient person; leaving but four cases in eleven years among those who could be properly called residents.

Q. Has Johnson's Island ever had a bad repute for unhealthiness?

A. I have never heard Johnson's Island called unhealthy.

Q. Have you ever known any very fatal diseases among the inhabitants of Lake Erie?

A. The Asiatic cholera has passed through the lake region as an epidemic four times, I think, since it first made its appearance on this continent in 1832. I am not aware of any other very fatal diseases having prevailed in the lake region since my first acquaintance with it in 1830.

STATE OF OHIO, Erie County, { s. s.

Before me, the subscriber, a Notary Public in and for the County of Erie and State of Ohio, personally came G. C. Huntington, who, being duly sworn by me according to law, deposes and says that the statements above made are compiled from official and other reliable data, and that they are true according to his knowledge and belief.

GEO. C. HUNTINGTON.

Subscribed and sworn to before me, July 4th, A. D. 1864.
[SEAL.] A. S. KELLEY,
Notary Public.

EVIDENCE OF SOLDIERS OF THE REBEL ARMY CONFINED AT UNITED STATES STATIONS.

Testimony taken at Lincoln Hospital, Washington, D. C., taken June 4, 1864.

COMMISSIONERS PRESENT.— Dr. Wallace, Mr. Walden.

WILLIAM H. FERGUSON; 11th Mississippi infantry, twenty-six years old; private in Confederate service three years; health good while in service and up to the time of my capture.

Had walled tents sometimes, and some sometimes when in winter quarters.

Always had this kind of covering except while in active service; then we had no tents or cabins, say from first of May till we go into winter quarters.

We commonly carry one blanket. Could have more if we wanted it.

Could take captured tents and carry and use them if we chose.

We were comfortable as far as body clothing and blankets are concerned; when one coat or pants wears out we can get more from our own quartermasters.

A day's ration is one and one-eighth pounds wheat flour or one and one fourth pounds corn meal · one and one-fourth pounds beef, fresh (could generally get fresh beef, driving cattle along with us), or half-pound bacon in place of beef; we also drew during the first year of war, coffee, sugar, and rice; second and third years had no coffee; sometimes we could get sugar and rice; since Christmas last we got coffee again.

We always had plenty to eat and sometimes more, while not on campaign; but on campaign, then we always had enough, but none to spare.

Since our capture we get enough grub to keep us from hunger; we don't suffer; we have a full allowance; we are as well treated as your own men.

I was wounded in my right leg just above the ankle; healing kindly now.

Kindly treated by the officers and subordinates since our capture.

I have not been, and never have seen any of our boys, robbed or otherwise ill-treated by the Union men; I have seen and heard some occasional rough talk and swearing at us, but nothing more than that; this was from a few of the privates; not a general rule.

We have had civil talk and argument as a common thing with the Union soldiers on the subject of the war.

I was captured 5th of May, 1864.

Our food in the Confederate army was of good quality.

Our corn meal that we had was very good; we had generally white, sometimes yellow meal; it was bolted or sifted, and of fine grain.

We never had grains of corn or bits of cob in our meal.

WILLIAM H. FERGUSON,
Company D, 11th Mississippi Volunteers.

I have been in the Confederate service two years and six months; was captured on fifth of May, 1864. Was wounded through the right shoulder and chest. I am improving in strength; and I suppose I am gaining flesh now, though I am not as strong or fleshy as when I was captured.

I have been present at the statements made by William H. Ferguson, 11th Mississippi Volunteers; I have heard them all; I substantiate their accuracy from my experience and observation as to our condition in the service, though I was attached to a different corps of the army.

W. O. QUARLES,
Company H, 3d Alabama Regiment, Infantry.

LARKIN A. GRIFFIN, native of South Carolina; home in Florida; belong to 1st South Carolina rifles.

The statement made by William H. Ferguson has been read and shown to me. It agrees with my observation and experience except as noted below. I have been in Confederate service nearly three years; my health was always excellent while in the service; I was well and strong when wounded and captured; captured on 12th May, 1864.

During the winter of 1862 and 1863, we had full rations of bread, but only half rations of bacon for about three months.

Our corn meal was very finely ground, but the hull was not sifted out.

In a few isolated cases our captured men were directed to leave their knapsacks and haversacks behind them; it was not a general thing at all.

I never saw nor heard our men sworn at or cursed by the Union soldiers.

L. A. GRIFFIN.

I have seen and had read to me the statements made by William H. Ferguson. They are correct as proved by my own experience and observation generally. I have been in the Confederate service three years; my health and strength while in the service was good during the third year; better than before.

We had coffee always, except during 1863, up to about Christmas.

A Union lieutenant once damned me and told me I was not worthy of a place. I replied, "I hoped the Lord would forgive him and make him a better man."

PLEASANT H. REESE,
Company I, 13th Georgia Regiment.

I have seen and had read to me the statements made by William H. Ferguson. They are correct as proved by my own experience and observation generally. I have been in the Confederate service two years; my health was not very good till this last winter; then it was tolerably good; could do all my duties. Through last summer we did not draw coffee.

JOSEPH F. DAVIDSON,
Company A, 49th Georgia Regiment.

VIRGIL CARROLL, aged twenty-one; artillery, Virginia.

Clothing always good and warm.

Plenty of blankets and good shelter; shelter tents.

Plenty to eat. Rations — coffee, sugar, bacon, meal, occasionally fresh meat, potatoes (Irish), rice, peas, wheat bread.

Always enough; much as we could consume; this especially during the last three months.

Clothing very plentiful.

Fourth year in the army; never suffered for food or clothing.

VIRGIL CARROLL.

I corroborate the above statement of Virgil Carroll. S. P. TWEDY.
Company C, 11th Regiment, Virginia.

JOSHUA BARKER, South Carolina, 4th Rifles. I corroborate the above statement of Virgil Carroll. JOSHUA BARKER.

C. A. BOWMAN, North Carolina 32d. I corroborate the above statement of Virgil Carroll. C. A. BOWMAN.

DISTRICT OF COLUMBIA, } ss.
County of Washington,

Personally appeared before me the within named William H. Ferguson, W. O. Quarles, L. A. Griffin, Pleasant H. Reese, Joseph F. Davidson, Virgil Carroll, S. P. Twedy, Joshua Barker, C. A. Bowman, who, being severally sworn, say that the statements set forth by them are correct and true to the best of their knowledge and belief.

Given under my hand and seal at Washington, D.C., this fourth day of June, A. D. 1864.

M. H. N. KENDIG,
Notary Public.

Testimony taken at De Camp General Hospital, U.S. A., New York, June 17, 1864.

COMMISSIONER PRESENT:— Mr. Wilkins.

Deposition of A. B. BARRON, of Habersham county, Georgia, Co. K, 24th Georgia.

I have served in the Confederate service two years and three days. I arrived at this hospital two days since, and depose as follows:

That I have served in Virginia, and was wounded at Cool Arbor.

I the Confederate service we had no tents in the field, except shelter tents; had one blanket and one oil-cloth, and lay on the ground.

When wounded, had on a good suit and a change of clothes, but was not robbed of money, clothes, or anything which I had when taken captive.

To-morrow being the last day of the week, and the time for a regular supply of clothing, I expect clean clothes. Everything was in a proper state for my reception when I arrived here.

I have been in the Confederate hospitals in the field; there were straw beds and a few sheets.

Rations in our service were bacon, half pound, or one pound of beef; rice, coffee and sugar occasionally; rations of bread were six hard biscuit a day, or half pound of meal or flour a day.

We had a plentiful supply of wood; our people did not suffer from cold.

We had medical attendance and medicines as we had need.

The sick were treated kindly; there was care as to our cleanliness; it was the best; soap, &c., was issued to us; no want of salt.

Since we were captured, we have been treated very well, just as well as your own boys all the time, and we have no fault to find. I was told I could not find it so.

I was a farmer; worked on my father's farm. I expected to be made a conscript, and volunteered in preference.

ALBERT B. BARRON.

Sworn to before me,
WARREN WEBSTER,
Assistant Surgeon U. S. A., in charge of Hospital.

Deposition of WM. M. FARMER, native of Franklin county, Georgia, Company H, 24th Georgia Regiment. Business, a farmer.

I entered the service of the Confederate States in August, 1861; was wounded and taken prisoner at Cool Arbor.

I had on, when wounded, a waistcoat, pants, drawers, shirt and boots, and not anything was taken away from me by my captors.

I have needed nothing since captured, having been supplied at the landing by the Sanitary Commission. I have had plenty to eat; no difference has been made since my capture between the wounded prisoners and the Federal wounded.

Rations in our service were bacon, half pound, or half pound of beef; rice, coffee and sugar occasionally; rations of bread were six hard biscuit a day, or half pound of meal, or half pound of flour a day. I have always had food enough of this kind, and while in Virginia the same as elsewhere.

In the Confederate service we had good tents in the winter, but on the march we had only blankets, and no shelter.

I was in No. 4 General Hospital, Richmond, during sixteen days, in May 1863; we had there as much as we could eat, with good bedding and sheets as we have here.

We were better off in the hospital than in the field, as we had there coffee, sugar and soft bread.

I have had every comfort and attention since I have been here. The same in all respects as Union soldiers.

WILLIAM M. FARMER.

Sworn to before me,
WARREN WEBSTER,
Assistant Surgeon U.S. A., in charge of Hospital.

Deposition of DANIEL F. PRINCE, native of Columbus county, North Carolina, Company H, 51st Regiment.

I entered the Confederate service in March, 1862, and arrived here on the 15th of June last. I was wounded at the battle of Cool Arbor; had some extra clothing in a bundle, which was cut loose by a Federal soldier at my request.

I lay in a cross fire, and the Federal soldiers dragged me out of the line of the fire into a ditch.

I was treated mighty kindly.

The Federals dressed my wounds, and carried me to White House Landing, and sent me immediately North with your own boys.

In the Confederate service we always got one pound of beef or half a pound of bacon a day; we had flour or corn bread alternately, one pound of flour, or one and a quarter pounds of corn meal; we had no tea or coffee; we had salt, and a gill of peas or rice a day extra.

We had three full suits of clothes a year, if needed; if more, we drew them and had to pay for them; we had blankets and oil-cloths.

We had tents at stations, but no tents in the field.

We had overcoats in cold weather made of wool.

I have been supplied with everything I have wanted since I came here, and see no difference between my treatment and that of Union soldiers here in the hospital.

DANIEL F. ^{his} ✗ _{mark.} PRINCE.

Sworn to before me,
WARREN WEBSTER,
Assistant Surgeon U. S. A., in charge of Hospital.

Deposition of JOSEPH WHICHARD, Pitt County, North Carolina, Company G, 8th Regiment, North Carolina.

I entered the service in September, 1861, and have served in North Carolina, South Carolina, Georgia, and at last in Virginia, where I was wounded at Cool Arbor.

I had on at the time, pants, shoes, a shirt, and a pair of drawers; my clothes were cut off by the surgeon in order to dress my wounds, and clean ones were afterwards supplied to me by Union men, both on board the boat and since I have been here.

I have my jacket, and the rest of my property is on the *little stand* at the *head of my bed*.

A blanket was taken away from me when wounded, but another has been furnished.

Rations, half a pound bacon, and ten hard biscuits, daily; nothing else to eat; no rice, peas, or corn meal.

Was in the hospital at Wilmington, North Carolina, a year ago last May. The fare was tolerable.

On a march, had an abundance, except for a day or two, when it could not be got.

Have had everything I want, or have asked for, since I have been here.

J. WHICHARD.

Sworn to before me,
WARREN WEBSTER,
Assistant Surgeon U. S. A. in charge of Hospital.

Deposition of MICHAEL SUTTON, Sampson County, North Carolina, Company B, 51st Regiment.

I have been nearly three years in the Confederate service; this is my second enlistment; I might have been drafted if I had not re-enlisted. I served near Charlestown, South Carolina, and was wounded at Cool Arbor; had some clothes on; no clothes now except what was furnished me by Union men; my own clothes were bloody and bad to be thrown away.

I have not been robbed of anything.

Rations for four days, one pound of bacon, and eighteen ounces of corn meal; same weight of flour, but rarely; had rice and peas, half pint of rice, and a short half pint of peas a day. Meal not always good, but lumpy and smelt bad, and then we were rather stinted for food. Since we have been 'round Richmond we have been short; it was enough to live upon "without enough."

Been in hospital in Wilmington, North Carolina; "fare awful hard;" want of food; beds, &c., were clean.

Treated well on board the vessel; the same as Union soldiers; kind and attentive here; fared fine while I have been here; I have not asked for anything but what I have got it.

MICHAEL ^{his} ✗ _{mark.} SUTTON.

Sworn to before me,
WARREN WEBSTER,
Assistant Surgeon U. S. A., in charge of hospital.

Testimony taken at Fort Delaware, June 21st, 1864.

COMMISSIONERS PRESENT. — Dr. Wallace, Judge Hare.

GEORGE S. ROLER *sworn and examined:*—

I am from Virginia; was in the artillery, Ewell's Corps; I am comfortable here; I have just come here last evening; came through Washington, from Spottsylvania Court House, where I was taken prisoner.

Was kindly treated on the way up; had been in the service (Confederate) three months when taken prisoner.

We had plenty of rations from Confederate Government; they issued us meal, some flour, bacon, sugar, coffee and salt; got meat every day, half pound bacon or a pound of beef; one and one-eighth pound of meal a day, which we made ourselves; plenty of coffee and sugar all the winter; we did not suffer for want of food.

Clothing plenty all winter; that was the case of the other men as well as myself; we all had two blankets—some more; none I think less than two.

GEORGE S. ROLER.

Sworn to and subscribed before me,
June 21st, 1864.
D. P. BROWN, JR.,
United States Commissioner.

HENRY DANIEL, *sworn and examined:*—

I have been in the Confederate service, infantry, Ewell's corps, for two years; I came here yesterday; taken prisoner at Spottsylvania; am from Georgia.

Had plenty to eat while in the Confederate service; had half pound of bacon, one and one-eighth pounds of flour a day during the winter; in the spring, beef one pound a day; provisions of good quality; besides this had meal, Irish potatoes, peas, coffee, and sugar.

Had clothes enough to keep warm; two blankets, one overcoat; the army at large had them; nothing to complain of in the way of food and clothing.

his
HENRY ✕ DANIEL.
mark.

Sworn to and subscribed before me,
June 21st, 1864.
D. P. BROWN, JR.,
United States Commissioner.

WILLIAM SHARP, *sworn and examined:*—

I have been three years in the Confederate service the 9th of next month, in Hill's corps; I am from Georgia; taken prisoner at Spottsylvania.

Treatment was not so good part of the way coming up here; they did not give us anything to eat but four crackers a day till we got to Belle Plain, to the boat; after that we had plenty; the guards that were with us across to Belle Plain did not get it either; the infantry guard that fetched us to Fredericksburg had no more than we; the cavalry brought us, I don't know how they fared.

Rations last winter in the Confederate service pretty good; got one and one-eighth pounds of flour, one-quarter pound of salt pork, when we got sugar and coffee; when we did not get sugar and coffee, had half a pound salt pork; sometimes we drew corn meal and got a pound and a quarter of it; got some potatoes once and a while; some beans occasionally, and some rice.

Clothes were very good last winter; had one blanket to each man; some had two blankets; had overcoats.

Heard no complaints of want of food or clothing, being well clothed and fed.

I was as fat as I ever was in my life, when I was taken at Spottsylvania.

We had tents and cabins built during the winter.

his
WILLIAM ✕ SHARP.
mark.

Sworn to and subscribed before me, June 21st, 1864.
D. P. BROWN, JR.,
United States Commissioner.

J. S. MOORE, *sworn and examined:*—

I have been in the Confederate service nearly three years. Taken prisoner near Spottsylvania Court House; was treated tolerably well on the way up here; did not get quite enough to eat.

Plenty to eat last winter and spring in the Confederate service; got meal, flour, bacon, a quarter of a pound of bacon a day, and one and one-quarter pounds of meal, sometimes sugar and coffee and potatoes; did not get beans; got no fresh meat last spring. Was in Hill's corps.

Had plenty of clothing; one blanket a piece; overcoats; some had two blankets.

We could not carry more than one blanket a piece; could have had more if we had chosen to carry them.

Sometimes we threw them away.

I came from Mississippi.

Sometimes drew flour, one pound, instead of meal; never got any more bacon than at first; had plenty to eat all the time; generally had coffee on hand all the time; used to have peas last fall; was as well fed, with the exception of coffee, last winter as before.

JOHN S. MOORE.

Sworn to and subscribed before me, June 21st, 1864.
D. P. BROWN, JR.,
United States Commissioner.

L. S. CREWS, *sworn and examined:*—

I entered the Confederate service last December. I was taken prisoner near Spottsylvania Court House; came from Virginia; in Ewell's corps; well treated coming up here; got more than I could eat, for I was sick; they all got plenty coming up here, as far as I know.

Rations last winter in our own army were tolerable; was on corn meal principally through the winter; got one and one-quarter pound of corn meal a day, half pound of bacon; sometimes molasses and potatoes; some fish, some sugar and coffee; drawed a little rice; got no fresh meat; had a little last December; had enough food to satisfy hunger.

The men were clothed tolerably well — all of the men had not blankets; some had thrown them away; it was so with the overcoats. I was conscripted.

his
L. S. ✕ CREWS.
mark.

Sworn to and subscribed before me,
June 21st, 1864.
D. P. BROWN, JR.,
United States Commissioner.

R. D. BENEFIELD, sworn and examined:—
Taken prisoner near Spottsylvania; was well treated, as well as could be expected on my way up here.

Got about enough to eat in the Confederate service — one and one-quarter pounds of meal, and one-quarter pound of bacon; got some sugar, some potatoes, rice, and coffee; no beans or peas; some sugar; allowance of bacon the same all the time; I don't recollect drawing any fresh meat; got flour sometimes.

Got tolerable plenty of clothes; all had plenty of blankets; some overcoats.

The men did not suffer, as I know of, from cold; have been in the service since February, 1861. Was in Ewell's corps.
R. D. BENEFIELD,
Company A, 37th Georgia.

Sworn to and subscribed before me,
June 21st, 1864.
D. P. BROWN, JR.,
United States Commissioner.

I certify that the foregoing testimony, taken at Fort Delaware, June 21st, 1864, was taken and reduced to writing by me, in the presence of the respective witnesses, and by them sworn to and subscribed in my presence, at the time and in the manner set forth.
D. P. BROWN, JR.,
United States Commissioner.

SUPPLEMENT.

SUFFERINGS OF THE PRISONERS AT ANDERSONVILLE, GA.—MEMORIAL FROM THE PRISONERS TO THE PRESIDENT OF THE UNITED STATES—LETTER OF MAJOR-GENERAL BUTLER, UNITED STATES COMMISSIONER OF EXCHANGE, TO COLONEL OULD, CONFEDERATE COMMISSIONER.

Account of the sufferings of Union prisoners of war, at Camp Sumter, Andersonville, Georgia.

From the Sanitary Commission Bulletin.

The following statement was drawn up for the Commission, and sworn to by the parties signing it. They were exchanged on the 16th of August, and with three others were appointed by their companions in prison as a deputation to see President Lincoln in their behalf.

Deposition of PRIVATE TRACY:—

I am a private in the 82d New York Regiment of Volunteers, Company G. Was captured with about eight hundred Federal troops, in front of Petersburg, on the 22d of June, 1864. We were kept at Petersburg two days, at Richmond, Belle Isle, three days, then conveyed by rail to Lynchburg. Marched seventy-five miles to Danville, thence by rail to Andersonville, Georgia. At Petersburg we were treated fairly, being under the guard of old soldiers of an Alabama regiment; at Richmond we came under the authority of the notorious and inhuman Major Turner, and the equally notorious Home Guard. Our ration was a pint of beans, four ounces of bread, and three ounces of meat, a day. Another batch of prisoners joining us, we left Richmond sixteen hundred strong.

All blankets, haversacks, canteens, money, valuables of every kind, extra clothing, and in some cases the last shirt and drawers, had been previously taken from us.

At Lynchburg we were placed under the Home Guard, officered by Major and Captain Moffett. The march to Danville was a weary and painful one of five days, under a torrid sun, many of us falling helpless by the way, and soon filling the empty wagons of our train. On the first day we received a little meat, but the *sum* of our rations for the five days was thirteen crackers. During the six days by rail to Andersonville, meat was given us twice, and the daily ration was four crackers.

On entering the Stockade Prison, we found it crowded with twenty-eight thousand of our fellow-soldiers. By *crowded*, I mean that it was difficult to move in any direction without jostling and being jostled. This prison is an open space, sloping on both sides, originally seventeen acres, now twenty-five acres, in the shape of a parallelogram, without trees or shelter of any kind. The soil is sand over a bottom of clay. The fence is made of upright trunks of trees, about twenty feet high, near the top of which are small platforms, where the guards are stationed. Twenty feet inside and parallel to the fence is a light railing, forming the "dead line," beyond which the projection of a foot or finger is sure to bring the deadly bullet of the sentinel.

Through the ground, at nearly right-angles

PRISON AT ANDERSONVILLE, GEORGIA.

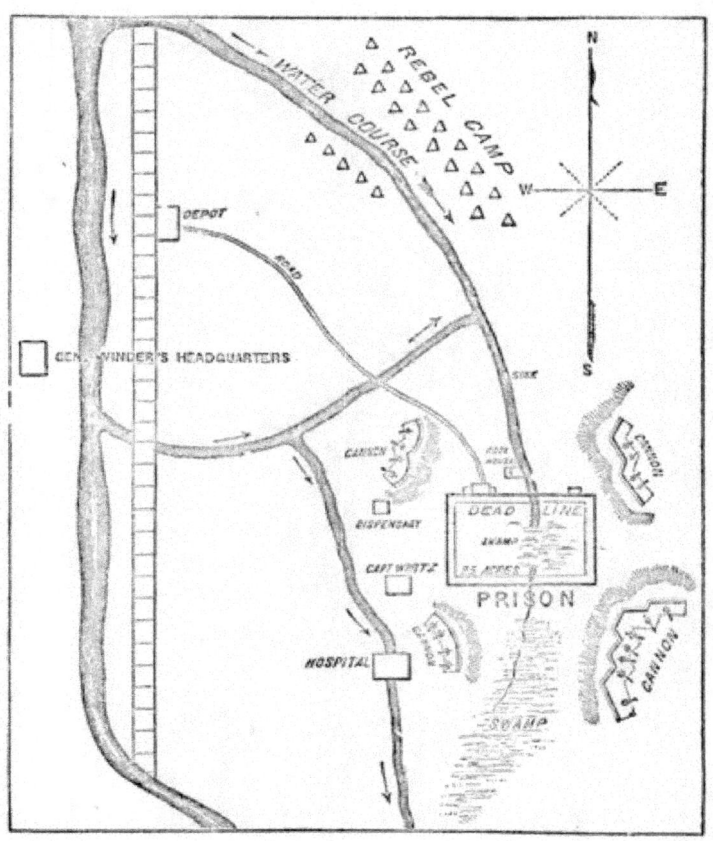

with the longer sides, runs or rather creeps a stream through an artificial channel, varying from five to six feet in width, the water about ankle deep, and near the middle of the enclosure, spreading out into a swamp of about six acres, filled with refuse wood, stumps and debris of the camp. Before entering this enclosure, the stream, or more properly sewer, passes through the camp of the guards, receiving from this source, and others farther up, a large amount of the vilest material, even the contents of the sink. The water is of a dark color, and an ordinary glass would collect a thick sediment. This was our only drinking and cooking water. It was our custom to filter it as best we could, through our remnants of haversacks, shirts and blouses. Wells had been dug, but the water either proved so productive of diarrhœa, or so limited in quantity that they were of no general use. The cook-house was situated on the stream just outside the stockade, and its refuse of decaying offal was thrown into the water, a greasy coating covering much of the surface. To these was added the daily large amount of base matter from the camp itself. There was a system of policing, but the means was so limited, and so large a number of the men was rendered irresolute and depressed by imprisonment, that the work was very imperfectly done. One side of the swamp was naturally used as a sink, the men usually going out some distance into the water. Under the summer sun this place early became corruption too vile for description, the men breeding disgusting life, so that the surface of the water moved as with a gentle breeze.

The new-comers, on reaching this, would exclaim: "Is this hell?" yet they soon would become callous, and enter unmoved the horrible rottenness. The rebel authorities never removed any filth. There was seldom any visitation by the officers in charge. Two surgeons were at one time sent by President DAVIS to inspect the camp, but a walk through a small section gave them all the information they desired, and we never saw them again.

The guards usually numbered about sixty-four — eight at each end, and twenty-four on a side. On the outside, within three hundred yards, were fortifications, on high ground, overlooking and perfectly commanding us, mounting twenty-four twelve-pound Napoleon Parrotts. We were never permitted to go outside, except at times, in small squads, to gather our firewood. During the building of the cook-house, a few, who were carpenters, were ordered out to assist.

Our only shelter from the sun and rain and night dews was what we could make by stretching over us our coats or scraps of blankets, which a few had, but generally there was no attempt by day or night to protect ourselves.

The rations consisted of eight ounces of corn bread (the cob being ground with the kernel), and generally sour, two ounces of condemned pork, offensive in appearance and smell. Occasionally, about twice a week, two tablespoonfuls of rice, and in place of the pork the same amount (two tablespoonfuls) of molasses were given us about twice a month.* This ration was brought into camp about four o'clock, P. M., and thrown from the wagons to the ground, the men being arranged in divisions of two hundred and seventy, subdivided into squads of nineties and thirties. It was the custom to consume the whole ration at once, rather than save any for the next day. The distribution being often unequal some would lose the rations altogether. We were allowed no dish or cooking utensil of any kind. On opening the camp in the winter, the first two thousand prisoners were allowed skillets, one to fifty men, but these were soon taken away. To the best of my knowledge, information and belief, our ration was in quality a starving one, it being either too foul to be touched or too raw to be digested.

The cook-house went into operation about May 10th, prior to which we cooked our own rations. It did not prove at all adequate to the work, (thirty thousand is a large town,) so that a large proportion were still obliged to prepare their own food. In addition to the utter inability of many to do this, through debility and sickness, we never had a supply of wood. I have often seen men with a little bag of meal in hand, gathered from several rations, starving to death for want of wood, and in desperation would mix the raw material with water and try to eat it.

The clothing of the men was miserable in the extreme. Very few had shoes of any kind, not two thousand had coats and pants, and those were late comers. More than one-half were indecently exposed, and many were naked.

The usual punishment was to place the men in the stocks, outside, near the Captain's quarters. If a man was missing at roll-call, the squad of ninety to which he belonged was deprived of the ration. The "dead-line" bullet, already referred to, spared no offend-

---

* Our regular army ration is:
¾ lb. Pork or 1¼ lbs. Fresh Beef,
18 ozs. Hard Bread, or 20 ozs. Soft Bread or Flour,
1-10 lb. Coffee,
1-6 lb. Sugar,
1-10 lb. Rice, or
1-10 lb. Beans or Hominy.
Vegetables — Fresh or Desiccated,
Molasses,
Vinegar.
} Irregularly.

er. One poor fellow, just from Sherman's army — his name was Roberts — was trying to wash his face near the "dead-line" railing, when he slipped on the clayey bottom, and fell with his head just outside the fatal border. We shouted to him, but it was too late — "another guard would have a furlough," the men said. It was a common belief among our men, arising from statements made by the guard, that General WINDER, in command, issued an order that any one of the guard who should shoot a Yankee outside of the "dead-line" should have a month's furlough, but there probably was no truth in this. About two a day were thus shot, some being cases of suicide, brought on by mental depression or physical misery, the poor fellows throwing themselves, or madly rushing outside the "line."

The mental condition of a large portion of the men was melancholy, beginning in despondency and tending to a kind of stolid and idiotic indifference. Many spent much time in arousing and encouraging their fellows, but hundreds were lying about motionless, or stalking vacantly to and fro, quite beyond any help which could be given them within their prison walls. These cases were frequent among those who had been imprisoned but a short time. There were those who were captured at the first Bull Run, July 1861, and had known Belle Isle from the first, yet had preserved their physical and mental health to a wonderful degree. Many were wise and resolute enough to keep themselves occupied — some in cutting bone and wood ornaments, making their knives out of iron hoops — others in manufacturing ink from the rust from these same hoops, and with rude pens sketching or imitating bank notes, or any sample that would involve long and patient execution.

Letters from home very seldom reached us, and few had any means of writing. In the early summer, a large batch of letters — five thousand we were told — arrived, having been accumulating somewhere for many months. These were brought into camp by an officer, under orders to collect ten cents on each — of course most were returned, and we heard no more of them. One of my companions saw among them three from his parents, but he was unable to pay the charge. According to the rules of transmission of letters over the lines, these letters must have already paid ten cents each to the rebel government.

As far as we saw General Winder and Captain Wirtz, the former was kind and considerate in his manners, the latter harsh, though not without kindly feelings.

It is a melancholy and mortifying fact, that some of our trials came from our own men. At Belle Isle and Andersonville there were among us a gang of desperate men, ready to prey on their fellows. Not only thefts and robberies, but even murders were committed. Affairs became so serious at Camp Sumter that an appeal was made to General Winder, who authorized an arrest and trial by a criminal court. Eighty-six were arrested, and six were hung, beside others who were severely punished. These proceedings effected a marked change for the better.

Some few weeks before being released, I was ordered to act as clerk in the hospital. This consists simply of a few scattered trees and fly tents, and is in charge of Dr. White, an excellent and considerate man, with very limited means, but doing all in his power for his patients. He has twenty-five assistants, besides those detailed to examine for admittance to the hospital. This examination was made in a small stockade attached to the main one, to the inside door of which the sick came or were brought by their comrades, the number to be removed being limited. Lately, in consideration of the rapidly increasing sickness, it was extended to one hundred and fifty daily. That this was too small an allowance is shown by the fact that the deaths within our stockade were from thirty to forty a day. I have seen one hundred and fifty bodies waiting passage to the "d ad house," to be buried with those who died in hospital. The average of deaths through the earlier months was thirty a day; at the time I left, the average was over one hundred and thirty, and one day the record showed one hundred and forty-six.

The proportion of deaths from starvation, not including those consequent on the diseases originating in the character and limited quantity of food, such as diarrhœa, dysentery and scurvy, I cannot state; but to the best of my knowledge, information and belief, there were scores every month. We could, at any time, point out many for whom such a fate was inevitable, as they lay or feebly walked, mere skeletons, whose emaciation exceeded the examples given in Leslie's Illustrated for June 18, 1864. For example: in some cases the inner edges of the two bones of the arms, between the elbow and the wrist, with the intermediate blood vessels, were plainly visible when held toward the light. The ration, in quantity, was perhaps barely sufficient to sustain life, and the cases of starvation were generally those whose stomachs could not retain what had become entirely indigestible.

For a man to find, on waking, that his comrade by his side was dead, was an occurrence too common to be noted. I have seen death in almost all the forms of the hospital and battle-field, but the daily scenes in Camp Sumter exceeded in the extremity of misery all my previous experience.

The work of burial is performed by our own men, under guard and orders, twenty-five bodies being placed in a single pit, without head-boards, and the sad duty performed with indecent haste. Sometimes our men were rewarded for this work with a few sticks of fire-wood, and I have known them to quarrel over a dead body for the job.

Dr. White is able to give the patients a diet but little better than the prison rations — a little flour porridge, arrow-root, whiskey and wild or hog tomatoes. In the way of medicine, I saw nothing but camphor, whiskey, and a decoction of some kind of bark — white oak, I think. He often expressed his regret that he had not more medicines. The limitation of military orders, under which the surgeon in charge was placed, is shown by the following occurrence: A supposed private, wounded in the thigh, was under treatment in the hospital, when it was discovered that he was a major of a colored regiment. The assistant-surgeon, under whose immediate charge he was, proceeded at once not only to remove him, but to kick him out, and he was returned to the stockade, to shift for himself as well as he could. Dr. White could not or did not attempt to restore him.

After entering on my duties at the hospital, I was occasionally favored with double rations and some wild tomatoes. A few of our men succeeded, in spite of the closest examination of our cloths, in secreting some green-backs, and with those were able to buy useful articles at exorbitant prices: — a tea-cup of flour at one dollar; eggs, three to six dollars a dozen; salt, four dollars a pound; molasses, thirty dollars a gallon; nigger beans, a small, inferior article, (diet of the slaves and pigs, but highly relished by us,) fifty cents a pint. These figures, multiplied by ten, will give very nearly the price in Confederate currency. Though the country abounded in pine and oak, sticks were sold to us at various prices, according to size.

Our men, especially the mechanics, were tempted with the offer of liberty and large wages to take the oath of allegiance to the Confederacy, but it was very rare that their patriotism, even under such a fiery trial, ever gave way. I carry this message from one of my companions to his mother: "My treatment here is killing me, mother, but I die cheerfully for my country."

Some attempts were made to escape, but wholly in vain, for, if the prison walls and guards were passed and the protecting woods reached, the bloodhounds were sure to find us out.

Tunneling was at once attempted on a large scale, but on the afternoon preceding the night fixed on for escape, an officer rode in and announced to us that the plot was discovered, and from our huge pen we could see on the hill above us the regiments just arriving to strengthen the guard. We had been betrayed. It was our belief that spies were kept in the camp, which could very easily be done.

The number in camp when I left was nearly thirty-five thousand, and daily increasing. The number in hospital was about five thousand. I was exchanged at Port Royal Ferry, August 16th.

PRESCOTT TRACY,
Eighty-second Regiment, N. Y. V.

City and County of New York, ss.

H. C. HIGGINSON and S. NOIROT, being duly sworn, say: That the above statement of Prescott Tracy, their fellow-prisoner, agrees with their own knowledge and experience.

H. C. HIGGINSON,
Co. K, Nineteenth Illinois Vols.
SILVESTER NOIROT,
Co. B, Fifth New Jersey Vols.

The Memorial of the Union Prisoners confined at Andersonville, Ga., to the President of the United States.

CONFEDERATE STATES PRISON,
CHARLESTON, S. C., August, 1864.

TO THE PRESIDENT OF THE UNITED STATES:

The condition of the enlisted men belonging to the Union armies, now prisoners to the Confederate rebel forces, is such that it becomes our duty, and the duty of every commissioned officer, to make known the facts in the case to the Government of the United States, and to use every honorable effort to secure a general exchange of prisoners, thereby relieving thousands of our comrades from the horror now surrounding them.

For some time past there has been a concentration of prisoners from all parts of the rebel territory to the State of Georgia — the commissioned officers being confined at Macon, and the enlisted men at Andersonville. Recent movements of the Union armies under General Sherman have compelled the removal of prisoners to other points, and it is now understood that they will be removed to Savannah, Georgia, and Columbus and Charleston, South Carolina. But no change of this kind holds out any prospect of relief to our poor men. Indeed, as the localities selected are far more unhealthy, there must be an increase rather than a diminution of suffering. Colonel Hill, provost marshal general, Confederate States army, at Atlanta, stated to one of the undersigned that there were thirty-five thousand prisoners at Andersonville, and by all accounts from the United States soldiers who have been confined there the number is not overstated by him. These thirty-five thousand are confined in a field of some thirty acres, enclosed by a board fence, heavily guarded. About one-third have various kinds of indifferent shelter; but upwards of thirty thousand are wholly without shelter, or even shade of any kind, and are exposed to the storms and rains, which are of almost daily occurrence; the cold dews of the night, and the more terrible effects of the sun striking with almost tropical fierceness upon their unprotected heads. This mass of men jostle and crowd each other up and down the limits of their enclosure, in storms or sun, and others lie down upon the pitiless earth at night with no other covering than the clothing upon their backs, few of them having even a blanket.

Upon entering the prison every man is deliberately stripped of money and other property, and as no clothing or blankets are ever supplied to their prisoners by the rebel authorities, the condition of the apparel of the soldiers, just from an active campaign, can be easily imagined. Thousands are without pants or coats, and hundreds without even a pair of drawers to cover their nakedness.

To these men, as indeed to all prisoners, there is issued three-quarters of a pound of bread or meal, and one-eighth of a pound of meat per day. This is the entire ration, and upon it the prisoner must live or die. The meal is often unsifted and sour, and the meat such as in the North is consigned to the soapmaker. Such are the rations upon which Union soldiers are fed by the rebel authorities, and by which they are barely holding on to life. But to starvation, and exposure to sun and storm, add the sickness which prevails to a most alarming and terrible extent. On an average, one hundred die daily. It is impossible that any Union soldier should know all the facts pertaining to this terrible mortality, as they are not paraded by the rebel authorities. Such statement as the following, made by —— ——, speaks eloquent testimony. Said he: "Of twelve of us who were captured, six died, four are in the hospital, and I never expect to see them again. There are but two of us left." In 1862, at Montgomery, Alabama, under far more favorable circumstances, the prisoners being protected by sheds, from one hundred and fifty to two hundred were sick from diarrhœa and chills, out of seven hundred. The same per centage would give seven thousand sick at Andersonville. It needs no comment, no efforts at word painting, to make such a picture stand out boldly in most horrible colors.

Nor is this all. Among the ill-fated of the many who have suffered amputation in consequence of injuries received before capture, sent from rebel hospitals before their wounds were healed, there are eloquent witnesses of the barbarities of which they are victims. If to these facts is added this, that nothing more demoralizes soldiers and develops the evil passions of man than starvation, the terrible condition of Union prisoners at Andersonville can be readily imagined. They are fast losing hope, and becoming utterly reckless of life. Numbers, crazed by their sufferings, wander about in a state of idiocy; others deliberately cross the "dead line," and are remorselessly shot down.

In behalf of these men we most earnestly appeal to the President of the United States. Few of them have been captured except in the front of battle, in the deadly encounter, and only when overpowered by numbers. They constitute as gallant a portion of our armies as carry our banners any where. If released, they would soon return to again do vigorous battle for our cause. We are told that the only obstacle in the way of exchange is the status of enlisted negroes captured from our armies, the United States claiming that the cartel covers all who serve under its flag, and the Confederate States refusing to consider the colored soldiers, heretofore slaves, as prisoners of war.

We beg leave to suggest some facts bearing upon the question of exchange, which we would urge upon this consideration. Is it not consistent with the national honor, without waiving the claim that the negro soldiers shall be treated as prisoners of war, to effect an exchange of the white soldiers? The two classes are treated differently by the enemy. The whites are confined in such prisons as Libby and Andersonville, starved and treated with a barbarism unknown to civilized nations. The blacks, on the contrary, are seldom imprisoned. They are distributed among the citizens, or employed on government works. Under these circumstances they receive enough to eat, and are worked no harder than they have been accustomed to be. They are neither starved or killed off by the pestilence in the dungeons of Richmond and Charleston. It is true they are again made slaves; but their slavery is freedom and happiness compared with the cruel existence imposed upon our gallant men. They are not bereft of hope, as are the white soldiers, dying by piece-meal. Their chances of escape are tenfold greater than those of the white soldiers, and their condition, in all its lights, is tolerable in comparison with that of the prisoners of war now languishing in the dens and pens of Secession.

While, therefore, believing the claims of our Government, in matters of exchange, to be just, we are profoundly impressed with the conviction that the circumstances of the two classes of soldiers are so widely different that the Government can honorably consent to an exchange, waiving for a time the established principle justly claimed to be applicable in the case. Let thirty-five thousand suffering, starving, and enlisted men aid this appeal. By prompt and decided action in their behalf, thirty-five thousand heroes will be made happy. For the eighteen hundred commissioned officers now prisoners we urge nothing. Although desirous of returning to our duty, we can bear imprisonment with more fortitude if the enlisted men, whose sufferings we know to be intolerable, were restored to liberty and life.

Letter of Major-General Butler, United States Commissioner of Exchange, to Col. Ould, the Confederate Commissioner.

HEADQUARTERS DEPARTMENT OF
VIRGINIA AND NORTH CAROLINA,
IN THE FIELD, *August* —, 1864.

HON. ROBERT OULD,
  Commissioner of Exchange.

SIR: — Your note to Major Mulford, Assistant Agent of Exchange, under date of 10th August, has been referred to me.

You therein state that Major Mulford has several times proposed " to exchange prisoners respectively held by the two belligerents, officer for officer and man for man," and that " the offer has also been made by other officials having charge of matters connected with the exchange of prisoners," and that " this proposal has been heretofore declined by the Confederate authorities." That you now " consent to the above proposition, and agree to deliver to you (Major Mulford) the prisoners held in captivity by the Confederate authorities, provided you agree to deliver an equal number of officers and men. As equal numbers are delivered from time to time, they will be declared exchanged. This proposal is made with the understanding that the officers and men on both sides who have been longest in captivity will be first delivered, where it is practicable."

From a slight ambiguity in your phraseology, but more, perhaps, from the antecedent action of your authorities, and because of your acceptance of it, I am in doubt whether you have stated the proposition with entire accuracy.

It is true, a proposition was made both by Major Mulford and by myself, as Agent of Exchange, to exchange all prisoners of war taken by either belligerent party, man for man, officer for officer, of equal rank, or their equivalents. It was made by me as early as the first of the winter of 1863–64, and has not been accepted. In May last I forwarded to you a note, desiring to know whether the Confederate authorities intended to treat colored soldiers of the United States army as prisoners of war. To that inquiry no answer has yet been made. To avoid all possible misapprehension or mistake hereafter as to your offer now, will you now say whether you mean by " prisoners held in captivity," colored men, duly enrolled, and mustered into the service of the United States, who have been captured by the Confederate forces; and if your authorities are willing to exchange all soldiers so mustered into the United States army, whether colored or otherwise, and the officers commanding them, man for man, officer for officer?

At the interview which was held between yourself and the Agent of Exchange on the part of the United States, at Fortress Monroe, in March last, you will do me the favor to remember the principal discussion turned upon this very point; you, on behalf of the Confederate Government, claiming the right to hold all negroes, who had heretofore been slaves, and not emancipated by their masters, enrolled and mustered into the service of the United States, when captured by your forces, not as prisoners of war, but upon capture to be turned over to their supposed masters or claimants, whoever they might be, to be held by them as slaves.

By the advertisements in your newspapers, calling upon masters to come forward and claim these men so captured, I suppose that your authorities still adhere to that claim — that is to say, that whenever a colored soldier of the United States is captured by you, upon whom any claim can be made by any person residing within the States now in insurrection, such soldier is not to be treated as a prisoner of war, but is to be turned over to his supposed owner or claimant, and put at such labor or service as that owner or claimant may choose, and the officers in command of such soldiers, in the language of a supposed act of the Confederate States, are to be turned over to the Governors of States, upon requisitions, for the purpose of being punished by the laws of such States, for acts done in war in the armies of the United States.

You must be aware that there is still a proclamation by Jefferson Davis, claiming to be Chief Executive of the Confederate States, declaring in substance that all officers of colored troops mustered into the service of the United States were not

THIRD SERIES. LIVING AGE. VOL. XXVII. 1265.

to be treated as prisoners of war, but were to be turned over for punishment to the Governors of States.

I am reciting these public acts from memory, and will be pardoned for not giving the exact words, although I believe I do not vary the substance and effect.

These declarations on the part of those whom you represent yet remain unrepealed, unannulled, unrevoked, and must, therefore, be still supposed to be authoritative.

By your acceptance of our proposition, is the Government of the United States to understand that these several claims, enactments, and proclaimed declarations are to be given up, set aside, revoked, and held for nought by the Confederate authorities, and that you are ready and willing to exchange man for man those colored soldiers of the United States, duly mustered and enrolled as such, who have heretofore been claimed as slaves by the Confederate States, as well as by white soldiers?

If this be so, and you are so willing to exchange these colored men claimed as slaves, and you will so officially inform the Government of the United States, then, as I am instructed, a principal difficulty in effecting exchanges will be removed.

As I informed you personally, in my judgment, it is neither consistent with the policy, dignity, or honor of the United States, upon any consideration, to allow those who, by our laws solemnly enacted, are made soldiers of the Union, and who have been duly enlisted, enrolled and mustered as such soldiers, who have borne arms in behalf of this country, and who have been captured while fighting in vindication of the rights of that country, not to be treated as prisoners of war, and remain unexchanged, and in the service of those who claim them as masters; and I cannot believe that the Government of the United States will ever be found to consent to so gross a wrong.

Pardon me if I misunderstood you in supposing that your acceptance of our proposition does not in good faith mean to include all the soldiers of the Union, and that you still intend, if your acceptance is agreed to, to hold the colored soldiers of the Union unexchanged, and at labor or service, because I am informed that very lately, almost contemporaneously with this offer on your part to exchange prisoners, and which seems to include *all* prisoners of war, the Confederate authorities have made a declaration that the negroes heretofore held to service by owners in the States of Delaware, Maryland, and Missouri are to be treated as prisoners of war, when captured in arms in the service of the United States.

Such declaration that a part of the colored soldiers of the United States were to be prisoners of war, would seem most strongly to imply that others were not to be so treated, or in other words, that the colored men from the insurrectionary States are to be held to labor and returned to their masters, if captured by the Confederate forces while duly enrolled and mustered into, and actually in the armies of the United States.

In the view which the Government of the United States takes of the claim made by you to the persons and services of these negroes, it is not to be supported upon any principle of national and municipal law.

Looking upon these men only as property upon your theory of property in them, we do not see how this claim can be made, certainly not how it can be yielded. It is believed to be a well-settled rule of public international law, and a custom and part of the laws of war, that the capture of movable property vests the title to that property in the captor, and therefore where one belligerent gets into full possession property belonging to the subjects or citizens of the other belligerent, the owner of that property is at once divested of his title, which rests in the belligerent Government capturing and holding such possession. Upon this rule of international law all civilized nations have acted, and by it both belligerents have dealt with all property, save slaves, taken from each other during the present war.

If the Confederate forces capture a number of horses from the United States, the animals are claimed to be, and, as we understand it, become the property of the Confederate authorities.

If the United States capture any movable property in the rebellion, by our regulations and laws, in conformity with international law, and the laws of war, such property is turned over to our Government as its property. Therefore, if we obtain possession of that species of property known to the laws of the insurrectionary States as slaves, why should there be any doubt that that property, like any other, vests in the United States?

If the property in the slave does so vest, then the "*jus disponendi*," the right of disposing of that property, vests in the United States.

Now, the United States have disposed of the property which they have acquired by capture in slaves taken by them, by giving that right of property to the man himself, to the slave, *i. e.* by emancipating him and declaring him free forever, so that if we have not mistaken the principles of international law and the laws of war, we have no slaves in the armies of the United States. All are free men, being made so in such manner as we have chosen to dispose of our property in them which we acquired by capture.

Slaves being captured by us, and the right of property in them thereby vested in us, that right of property has been disposed of by us by manumitting them, as has always been the acknowledged right of the owner to do to his slave. The manner in which we dispose of our property while it is in our possession certainly cannot be questioned by you.

Nor is the case altered if the property is not actually captured in battle, but comes either voluntarily or involuntarily from the belligerent owner into the possession of the other belligerent.

I take it no one would doubt the right of the United States to a drove of Confederate mules, or a herd of Confederate cattle, which should wander or rush across the Confederate lines into the lines of the United States army. So it seems to me, treating the negro as property merely, if that piece of property passes the Confederate lines, and comes into the lines of the United States, that property is as much lost to its owner in the Confederate States as would be the mule or ox, the property of the resident of the Confederate States, which should fall into our hands.

If, therefore, the privilege of international law and the laws of war used in this discussion are correctly stated, then it would seem that the deduction logically flows therefrom, in natural sequence, that the Confederate States can have no claim upon the negro soldiers captured by them from the armies of the United States, because of the former ownership of them by their citizens or subjects, and only claim such as result, under the laws of war, from their captor merely.

Do the Confederate authorities claim the right to reduce to a state of slavery free men, prisoners of war captured by them? This claim our fathers fought against under Bainbridge and Decatur, when set up by the Barbary Powers on the northern shore of Africa, about the year 1800, and in 1864 their children will hardly yield it upon their own soil.

This point I will not pursue further, because I understand you to repudiate the idea that you will reduce free men to slaves because of capture in war, and that you base the claim of the Confederate authorities to re-enslave our negro soldiers, when captured by you, upon the *"jus post liminī,"* or that principle of the law of nations which inhabilitates the former owner with his property taken by an enemy, when such property is recovered by the forces of his own country.

Or in other words, you claim that, by the laws of nations and of war, when property of the subjects of one belligerent power, captured by the forces of the other belligerent, is recaptured by the armies of the former owner, then such property is to be restored to its prior possessor, as if it had never been captured, and therefore, under this principle, your authorities propose to restore to their masters the slaves which heretofore belonged to them which you may capture from us.

But this post liminary right under which you claim to act, as understood and defined by all writers on national law, is applicable simply to *immovable property*, and that, too, only after complete resubjugation of that portion of the country in which the property is situated, upon which this right fastens itself. By the laws and customs of war, this right has never been applied to *movable* property.

True it is, I believe, that the Romans attempted to apply it to the case of slaves, but for two thousand years no other nation has attempted to set up this right as ground for treating slaves differently from other property.

But the Romans even refused to re-enslave men captured from opposing belligerents in a civil war, such as ours unhappily is.

Consistently then with any principle of the law of nations, treating slaves as property merely, it would seem to be impossible for the Government of the United States to permit the negroes in their ranks to be re-enslaved when captured, or treated otherwise than as prisoners of war.

I have forborne, sir, in this discussion, to argue the question upon any other or different ground of right than those adopted by your authorities in claiming the negro as property, because I understand that your fabric of opposition to the Government of the United States has the right of property in man as its corner-stone. Of course it would not be profitable in settling a question of exchange of prisoners of war to attempt to argue the question of abandonment of the very corner-stone of their attempted political edifice. Therefore I have admitted all the considerations which should apply to the negro soldier as a man, and dealt with him upon the Confederate theory of property only.

I unite with you most cordially, sir, in desiring a speedy settlement of all these questions, in view of the great suffering endured by our prisoners in the hands of your authorities, of which you so feelingly speak. Let me ask, in view of that suffering, why you have delayed eight months to answer a proposition which by now accepting you admit to be right, just, and humane, allowing that suffering to continue so long? One cannot help thinking, even at the risk of being deemed uncharitable, that the benevolent sympathies of the Confederate authorities have been lately stirred by the depleted condition of their armies, and a desire to get into the field, to affect the present campaign, the hale, hearty, and well-fed prisoners held by the United States in exchange for the half-starved, sick, emaciated, and unserviceable soldier of the United States now languishing in your prisons. The events of this war, if we did not know it before, have taught us that it is not the Northern portion of the American people alone who know how to drive sharp bargains.

The wrongs, indignities, and privations suffered by our soldiers would move me to consent to anything to procure their exchange, except to barter away the honor and faith of the Government of the United States, which has been so solemnly pledged to the colored soldiers in its ranks.

Consistently with national faith and justice we cannot relinquish this position. With your authorities it is a question of property merely. It seems to address itself to you in this form. Will you suffer your soldier, captured in fighting your battles, to be in confinement for months rather than release him by giving for him that which you call a piece of property, and which we are willing to accept as a man?

You certainly appear to place less value upon your soldier than you do upon your negro. I assure you, much as we of the North are accused of loving property, our citizens would have no difficulty in yielding up any piece of property they have in exchange for one of their brothers or sons languishing in your prisons. Certainly there could be no doubt that they would do so were that piece of property less in value than five thousand dollars in Confederate money, which is believed to be the price of an able-bodied negro in the insurrectionary States.

Trusting that I may receive such a reply to the questions propounded in this note, as will tend to a speedy resumption of the negotiations in a full exchange of all prisoners, and a delivery of them to their respective authorities,

I have the honor to be,
Very Respectfully,
Your Obedient Servant,
BENJAMIN F. BUTLER,
Major-General, and Commissioner of Exchange.

ALEXANDER H. STEPHENS AGAINST THE REBELLION.

There is an almost official confession of the "folly, wickedness, and madness" of the Rebellion, in a speech made by the so-called Vice-President, Alexander H. Stephens, in Georgia, in January, 1861, before it broke out, and made to prevent it. The whole speech has been often printed since. We have room only for a part.

"When we of the South demanded the slave-trade, or the importation of Africans for the cultivation of our lands, did they not yield the right for twenty years? When we asked a three-fifths representation in Congress for our slaves, was it not granted? When we asked and demanded the return of any fugitive from justice, or the recovery of those persons owing labor or allegiance, was it not incorporated in the Constitution, and again ratified and strengthened in the Fugitive Slave Law of 1850?

"But do you reply, that in many instances they have violated this compact, and have not been faithful to their engagements? As individuals and local communities they may have done so, but not by the sanction of government; for that has always been true to Southern interests. Again, gentlemen, look at another fact: When we have asked that more territory should be added, that we might spread the institution of Slavery, have they not yielded to our demands in giving us Louisiana, Florida, and Texas, out of which four States have been carved, and ample territory for four more to be added in due time, if you, by this unwise and impolite act, do not destroy this hope, and perhaps by it lose all, and have your last slave wrenched from you by stern military rule, as South America and Mexico were; or by the vindictive decree of a universal emancipation, which may reasonably be expected to follow?

"But, again, gentlemen, what have we to gain by this proposed change of our relation to the general government? We have always had the control of it, and can yet, if we remain in it, and are as united as we have been. We have had a majority of the Presidents chosen from the South, as well as the control and management of most of those chosen from the North. We have had sixty years of Southern Presidents to their twenty-four, thus controlling the Executive department. So of the judges of the Supreme Court, we have had eighteen from the South, and but eleven from the North; although nearly four-fifths of the judicial business has arisen in the Free States, yet a majority of the Court has always been from the South. This we have required, so as to guard against any interpretation of the Constitution unfavorable to us. In like manner we have been equally watchful to guard our interests in the Legislative branch of government. In choosing the presiding Presidents (pro tem.) of the Senate, we have had twenty-four to their eleven. Speakers of the House, we have had twenty-three, and they twelve. While the majority of the Representatives, from their greater population, have always been from the North, yet we have generally secured the Speaker, because he, to a great extent, shapes and controls the legislation of the country. Nor have we had less control in every other department of the general government. Attorney-generals we have had fourteen, while the North have had but five. Foreign ministers we have had eighty-six, and they but fifty four. While three-fourths of the business which demands diplomatic agents abroad is clearly from the Free States, from their greater commercial interests, yet we have had the principal embassies, so as to secure the world markets for our cotton, tobacco, and sugar, on the best possible terms. We have had a vast majority of the higher offices of both army and navy, while a larger proportion of the soldiers and sailors were drawn from the North. Equally so of clerks, auditors, and comptrollers filling the Executive department; the records show for the last fifty years, that of the three thousand thus employed, we have had more than two-thirds of the same, while we have but one-third of the white population of the Republic.

"Again, look at another item, and one, be assured, in which we have a great and vital interest; it is that of revenue, or means of supporting government. From official documents, we learn that a fraction over three-fourths of the revenue collected for the support of government has uniformly been raised from the North.

"Leaving out of view, for the present, the countless millions of dollars you must expend in a war with the North, with tens of thousands of your sons and brothers slain in battle, and offered up as sacrifices upon the altar of your ambition, — and for what, we ask again? Is it for the overthrow of the American government, established by our common ancestry, cemented and built up by their sweat and blood, and founded on the broad principles of *Right, Justice*, and *Humanity?* And, as such, I must declare here, as I have often done before, and which has been repeated by the greatest and wisest of statesmen and patriots in this and other lands, that *it is the best and freest government, the most equal in its rights, the most just in its decisions, the most lenient in its measures, and the most inspiring in its principles to elevate the race of men, that the sun of heaven ever shone upon.*

"Now, for you to attempt to overthrow such a government as this, under which we have lived for more than three-quarters of a century — in which we have gained our wealth, our standing as a nation, our domestic safety while the elements of peril are around us, with peace and tranquillity accompanied with unbounded prosperity and rights unassailed — is the height of madness, folly, and wickedness, to which I can neither lend my sanction nor my vote."

OFFICE OF LITTELL'S LIVING AGE, BOSTON.

Thank God that some, who have read that part of this report which was copied into the Living Age a fortnight ago, have submitted their minds to the accumulated proof of the horrible atrocity of the Rebellion, and the fiendish character of its leaders. It is to be hoped that this exposure, so able and so complete, made in such a calm, clear, and Christian spirit, will induce many to lay aside their life-long prejudice against any "interference with Southern institutions," — a prejudice so rooted as to have lasted even after the *sacred* INSTITUTION had openly made war against their country.

Since the publication of the former part, a subscriber, remitting payment for another year, says, "I am sorry to see The Living Age hoist the Black Abolition Flag." Look again, dear sir, as the mist clears off; it is not *black*: it is "Red, White and Blue;" "'Tis the Star-spangled Banner," the National Flag upheld by the President, by Congress, and by the nation.

The People of the United States, in the election which has just taken place, have manifested not only their fixed purpose to sustain the Government and nation which our fathers planted, with the blessing of God, but also to uphold the present administration in its slowly-matured determination to root out the *cause* which has placed them in peril.

The manner in which the war has been carried on by the rebels has been worthy of the object for which it was begun; and it is difficult to believe that any patriotic or humane man can hereafter be found acting with their Northern and European sympathizers.

The prefixed photographs show some few proofs of the enormous wickedness which these Accessories after the fact have to sanction.

www.ingramcontent.com/pod-product-compliance
Lightning Source LLC
Chambersburg PA
CBHW032239080426
42735CB00008B/929